GOD
OF THE
PÁRAMO

*Lessons Learned about Growing
God's Kingdom through Valuing Others*

MATTHEW L. BROOKS

WestBow
PRESS
A DIVISION OF THOMAS NELSON

WestBow Press books may be ordered through booksellers or by contacting:

WestBow Press
A Division of Thomas Nelson
1663 Liberty Drive
Bloomington, IN 47403
www.westbowpress.com
1-(866) 928-1240

ISBN: 978-1-4497-6881-2 (sc)
ISBN: 978-1-4497-6882-9 (hc)
ISBN: 978-1-4497-6880-5 (e)

Library of Congress Control Number: 2012918205

Printed in the United States of America

WestBow Press rev. date: 10/09/2012

To Guillermo and Lamar: Your investment in my life can't be measured. I can only hope these words do justice to what you have meant to me. Infinitas gracias!

To the people of Timotes: Thank you for receiving me as one of your own. You have been one of the greatest blessings God has had for me on this earth.

CONTENTS

Acknowledgments

I will forever remember Lamar as a man who sought to know others intimately. He could have easily dismissed me or held me at arm's length, like many Christians do with new visitors in church. He could have taken it upon himself to decide what good I could or could not be for the kingdom of God. Instead, his Christlike example changed the course of my life forever. He saw something in me even I wasn't able to see. That something, whatever it is, is in all of us, and God put it there.

There is a good chance Lamar is already enjoying his eternal reward. It's been several years since I've seen him and some time since I last tried to find out where and how he is. No one has heard from him. The certain thing is that God used him here on earth.

My close relationship with Lamar ended up leading me to Venezuela, and it has led me in an indirect way to Timotes. This adventure continues today because of what he sparked in my young life so many years ago. Please take some time to think about where your relationships are leading you.

The reason I continued to attend Mint Hill Baptist near Charlotte wasn't because of Lamar alone. I was experiencing tremendous spiritual growth there, and that was also because of Pastor Lee, the senior pastor there. He was a great husband and father who loved people and lived to serve God. It was great to shake his hand on the way out every Sunday just to get pulled in with his short arms for a loving embrace.

He was a very encouraging individual who also invited me to spend time with him besides Sunday services. He would invite me to lunch on occasion, and I also became part of the biweekly men's breakfast held at the fellowship hall of the church. Pastor Lee, who loved sports, was the chaplain for the Independence High School football team. He invited me a few times to go to games with him. We'd go into the locker room, he would introduce me to some of the players, and I'd stick around to hear his pre-game prayer, which was always powerful and full of emotion. Pastor Lee was a role model to those players and to me. He went to every Independence home game and knew a lot about football. He didn't inspire those kids just with his knowledge of the game; he inspired them by simply loving each and every one.

I have been blessed with great role models growing up. My father instilled in me the desire to work hard. My uncles taught me a lot about sports, a bit more about music, and a whole lot more about life. And my molecular biology professor, Dr. G, was the most demanding teacher I ever had but also the one who showed the most interest in my academic success and the one who got me to achieve like no other teacher had been able to. A role model has a way of getting the very best out of you, and the very best of us is what we should desire to give the Lord every day.

Having worked and lived in Venezuela for so many years, I never had to worry about a place to stay or a meal whenever I traveled anywhere in the country. People all over considered me their brother and would open their doors to me. It wasn't always in the middle of the afternoon when the sun was shining either. Many have opened their doors to me in the black and uncertain hours of the night. There are even people, such as Lubina, who actually kept a bedroom open for me in case I came. She knew I'd need a place to feel at home when I came to Cabimas to promote the Andean work. I found out on my first trip to Venezuela that Lamar had worked with Lubina's brother Mario for several years in Bolivia. This unexpected connection brought me closer to this special family.

Although I may have been in her home taking a break from my work, Lubina and her family still had to get up and go to work or school. It was something that convicted me but showed me love, seeing her up early preparing breakfast for me and doing my laundry. When I offered to help, it was almost as if I had offended her.

One thing that has been made very evident to me is that sacrifice is fueled by love. Love is what sent Jesus to the cross to die for us, and love is what motivates us to sacrifice certain things. What many people have taught me in my life is that sacrifice should be made for all people, not just friends and family.

I still pattern many things in my life after many of my blood relatives, but there have been many others not related by blood who have been used by God to mold me. Men such as Lamar, Pastor Lee, my Caracas supervisor Richard, Gordon, Pastor Angel, and Guillermo were as committed to helping me grow as a person and as a believer as anyone else. Love is so much more powerful when it crosses family lines.

These men just lived their lives in front of me. They didn't obligate me to do anything, but their love for me inspired me. When I submitted to the leadership of these men who have also molded me, I did it because their love for me was as pure as their walk. The most effective leaders in my life were not those who told me what to do but those who told me where God was leading them and invited me to come along. They also lovingly helped me eliminate the baggage I couldn't take with me.

I was living a mediocre Christian life when this story began, before I returned to church in Charlotte, North Carolina. I wasn't interested in profound spiritual truths; I was going to church just because it was what I thought I should be doing. Servants of God along the way helped me find purpose and fulfillment in my life, and worship on Sundays is now the best part of my week.

"To whomsoever much is given, of him shall be much required" (Luke 12:48) reminds me that God has given me much and that he expects my best in return. A position of influence requires a walk of greater integrity and gratitude. This passage also tells me I am where I am because of other people, and I need to reach out to others so they may find what God may have waiting for them as well.

Jesus told his disciples they would do greater things than even he had done. Jesus' love for his disciples inspired and motivated them. He did not want them to be stagnant. We should want the same for those we have been given influence over.

The men and women, brothers and sisters who have guided me in my life probably did so not even knowing they were influencing me. They did not assume control over my life; it was just a natural process on my part of being obedient. They saw me as part of their family, and they were used by God to guide me in his divine purpose for me. I see now how it should be done, and I know now that it depends on me paying it forward in the lives of others around me.

It is also important for me to acknowledge my sister Robin in relation to this book. We are contemporaries, and we shared many experiences growing up. She was a help to me in my first two semesters of seminary, when I was unsure if what I brought to the table academically would be enough to cut it. She encouraged me with the simple words, "You're an excellent writer, and I'm jealous." This was her way of letting me know I'd be just fine, but those words encouraged me like she will never know.

Bonnie, a coworker in Upstate New York, has been officially deemed my first fan. As I shared with her my growing desire to document my experiences overseas, she told me not only to "go for it" but spent many hours proofreading my work and just lending an ear as I mulled over the process of trying to get it published. Val, another coworker, gave great feedback as I began this process. She also shared many great ideas with me from novels and other examples of what she thought to be good writing.

This has been an incredible journey, and it's a story that needs to be told. One that could be possible only with an Almighty God, and I thank him every day for Venezuela and the gift it has been in my life. My prayer is that the words that follow will entertain you, help you reflect on your own experience, and give you yet another perspective on how great our God is.

—Matthew L. Brooks

My Life's Passion

The sun shone bright in the Carolina blue sky on that beautiful Thursday morning. I felt I'd arrived. All I'd ever wanted in life was to be on a golf course. That day I was working to get the course in shape for a nationally televised event. This was what I lived for—green-striped fairways and perfectly raked bunkers. This course was in its best shape ever; it was like a gift to all of us who had worked so hard. The long hours, from 4:00 a.m. until dark, were paying dividends. The sight before me was my reward for having worked my hands for hours on end, turning them into calloused, stiff appendages. Our attention to detail was being appreciated by everyone.

It was awesome to see the patrons out there enjoying themselves. It was almost as if they were coming to visit us. This place was my home; this was where I belonged. The main attractions that day, though, were the professional golfers who were competing in the Paine Webber Invitational in Charlotte, an event hosted by the king himself, Arnold Palmer.

As I set out early in the morning to bring water to the course for the players, I saw him. Arnold was not with his army (as the fans who followed him during his playing years was known) but riding alone. He too was giving the course a final inspection in his golf cart. He gave me a salute as he passed. What a special moment that was, to be recognized by the one and only Mr. Palmer! I thought life could not get much better than that. I was happy with myself, with my life choices, and with my profession.

Working for the PGA Tour was going to give me great references and work experience for future job searches. My resume was becoming more impressive by the day. I seemed to be in the right place at the right time. My future, and how bright it could be, was all up to me.

Golf has been my passion since I was a young kid. My uncles would include me in their foursomes; it was nice to be part of their outings. This led a few years later to my participation in summer-long youth golf tournaments that took us on a tour of the courses in Upstate New York. If my uncles had not invited me to play that first time, golf may not have become as big a part of my life as it is now.

I also remember being up in my room when I was a kid and supposedly working on school work, but all I did was draw golf holes on a sheet of paper, dreaming that one day I would design a golf course. This passion for golf course design led me to another opportunity to work on a new course in Charlotte from the day the trees were cleared from the land. One of the assistant superintendents from Piper Glen was leaving to head the project there and invited me to work with him. This would be the third golf course job for me in Charlotte, but each one had taught me more than the first. It was extremely hard work every day, cutting the paint-outlined greenside bunkers by hand. We cut all the drainage lines for all eighteen holes and laid the sod for the tees and greens.

It was much harder work than the job I'd had in golf course maintenance. This job, though, allowed me to see what a course looks like underneath the grass and sand. The intricate network of drainage lines and irrigation pipes and wires under the surface became something I got to know well. This was valuable experience that would hopefully help me land a job as a superintendent, which was my plan.

A golf course superintendent has a lot of responsibility but earns a very good wage. Having worked in the business for five years at that point, I was certain this was what I wanted. They always say the first step in life to getting somewhere is simply knowing where you're going.

My mother had eleven siblings, and each one had a special impact on my life; many things I'm passionate about today have come from time spent with them. My mother's brother Jim took me to my first rock and roll show, Jerry Lee Lewis, and we were seated next to the stage. I can still see that stage spinning as he jumped up and down on the piano.

I was very fortunate, too, that I had Uncle Jim as a sociology instructor in college. He took our class on a field trip to the legendary rock club CBGB's to see his son's band play. My taste in music is very eclectic because people such as Uncle Jim took the time to share new experiences with me. Uncle Jim also included me when a friend gave him tickets to see Michael Jordan and the Bulls play the Knicks in Madison Square Garden. It will be hard to ever forget that game; experiencing Jordan's talent live was far better than seeing it on television.

In life we are surrounded by invitations; some mold us, some test us, and some change us forever. Some invitations bring us closer to people, while others bring us closer to the God who created us. I was raised in a Christian home and did not stray far all through my teenage years. My sisters and I had a strong support system: a very close family. It was easy to stay on track with so many positive influences. I later found that even with so great a network of friends and family it is our intimacy with God that determines our futures and our successes.

The long days on the golf course did not bother me because I was raised with a good work ethic. My father made it very clear to me that my work was not done until every piece of wood he had chopped was neatly stacked. Even then I was in the process of learning how to do a job and how to do it right.

Certain memories of my father show me how our relationships mold us. It wasn't just the tangible things he did, like teaching me to work hard, to embrace my tasks and not be scared of them. It was everyday interactions that exposed me to things that are now an important part of my life.

One vivid memory from my childhood is having my father practice Spanish with me at the kitchen table. He was taking night classes at a community college and would come home speaking Spanish to me as part of his homework. The funny part was that I was actually able to converse with him.

I got my first paying job, stocking shelves at a grocery store, when I was sixteen. It was great punching in and out and getting paid for the time I put in. Having all my information on file with the company, like my social security number and address, was something all new and exciting, and it added a bit of seriousness to the matter. We were trained to stock shelves in a very specific way. The owners had a right to demand certain things since they were paying us. It was a good life lesson: do the job as you were taught to do it especially if you're being paid for it. My new friends and I became very fast and efficient workers. My schedule during my teen years was rigorous. Work four nights a week, participate in different sports throughout the school year, and of course complete all my homework.

I was raised to be a good person and to work hard. These things were good, but probably not enough to get me to eventually leave everything and move to another country to serve God. I did go off the straight and narrow path for a while until God's love brought me back. Throughout He reminded me that being good was a quality only He possessed, and no amount of work I did could make me good.

So far my story does not distinguish me from a lot of people. I was a normal, middle-of-the-road young person with a pretty normal life. A series of events would soon teach me that every single person on this planet has value to God, everyone from the sanctimonious religious zealot to people who don't yet seek to truly know Him.

Just a story about a young kid with a growing interest in sports and music may not be an overly compelling story. The story gets interesting when the young kid realizes that God uses people to fulfill His purposes, to reach desolate hearts, and to fill them with life and purpose.

Invitations

My work friends at the grocery store and I had a lot in common; we began to share more and more outside of work in the little free time we had. We'd play tackle football at the local elementary school to get our aggressions out (like any normal teenage boy would do after a busy week at school), we went bowling, and we also went to parties together. Any person, especially a teenager, will accept any invitation from a friend. So when I was invited to my first party with alcohol, it was something I didn't turn down. The party was at a friend's house, and I told my parents I'd been invited to sleep over there, with no mention of "party."

My first sip of beer was to me as the apple was to Adam and Eve. I'd always gone to church and was considered a good kid. I was baptized at eight and had been taught to live right. That party was a first for me, however, and it took me away from the things of God for several years.

The innocent decision to party carried over into my college years and became part of my life without me even realizing it. Like most sin, it gradually took control of me and grew. The seed had been planted by a simple invitation, one I wish I'd been wise enough to decline.

My last year of college in upstate New York was difficult. I was not motivated and was out at bars almost every night. There was always something about the sciences, though, that held my attention. To this day I still see things scientifically, analyzing everything around me and trying to understand it empirically. Biology was a fascinating subject, but how would I apply it in real life? Where would I work with a degree in the field? These are questions that haunt many college seniors, but the only advice we get is to find out what we love to do and go do it.

It would have been great to have taken my own advice back then and focused more on school because I was not focused at all. I was even less focused on the things of God. Spending so much time studying the sciences had me doubting the reality of God's existence anyway. Science was enough to help me understand the universe, and that in a way made it all right to spend so much time partying, since I was convincing myself I was not accountable to a higher power.

During one semester, for no particular reason some smart kids included me in their weekly study group. They were very bright individuals who excelled in every subject. I quickly learned that one of their secrets to success was that they absorbed facts from textbooks and retained them by repeating them over and over. This strategy allowed them to do well on exams, and I began to do the same. That semester I got decent grades for the first time in a long time.

During this time I was turned off by Christians who treated the Bible like college students do a textbook, that is, never making it real and turning people off by repeating the same things over and over. I know now the Bible is the living, breathing Word of God, but at that time it was just a book others encouraged me to read and believe. Albeit a book with good things in it, it was just a book. I now know God seeks a relationship with man because some very special people came into my life to seek a relationship with me. They didn't just preach to me; they invited me to be part of what God was doing all along.

Looking back, I see that we can't have an effective ministry until we experience God in a personal way. We can't just memorize and absorb Bible passages and regurgitate them as if we're taking a test. Relationships, not just knowledge, should move our ministries, and obedience makes them come alive.

The problem during my college years was that I had put the burden of my future in my own hands instead of trusting God. The carefree existence of a college student comes to a very quick end and it is replaced at once by the pressures of life. The choices of where to live, what job to take, or whether to continue school face every college graduate. It is amazing to me that I went through such a pivotal phase of my life walking so far from the Lord.

Finishing college with a degree in biology put a more merciful than deserving end to the disaster I'd made of it. Out every night at the bars and at parties, I hardly left myself time to get my homework done let alone excel in my studies. I had strayed far from what I was hoping to become and from what my family wanted me to be.

After graduation, I accepted an invitation from an uncle to test the job market in North Carolina. Uncle Tim had been in Charlotte for several years and had raised his two daughters there. He too was an avid golfer, and even living so far away he had a hand in growing my love for golf. The only thing he held against me was that I never became a fan of the New York Giants football team, the only New York–area team I don't root for.

Finding a job I loved in Charlotte with the prospect of it turning into a career gave me at least an idea of what I wanted to do with my life. I enrolled in a horticulture science program at a community college, planning on applying for golf course superintendent jobs. My Biology degree helped me, but this program was more specific. I learned the numerous species of turf grasses and plants as well as different soil types. The classes challenged me, but my time on the golf course taught me a lot. Fifteen-hour work days on the golf course were the norm, but it wasn't even like work. I loved every minute of it. With my whole life ahead of me, everything was working out.

This was a pivotal time for me. I'd met several friends from Upstate New York who lived in Charlotte, and we were spending a lot of time together. The scene in Uptown Charlotte was becoming more and more appealing, and seeing famous athletes in nightclubs on weekends was exciting, not anything I'd seen in my small town in New York. During this time I felt directly and indirectly judged by some Christians back home who pointed out my affinity for alcohol and nightlife, but this alone did not bring me back to church. It was the quiet voice inside my heart that was calling me back. I'm so glad I did go back; it eventually taught me what following Christ was all about.

After a few weeks living and working in Charlotte, I decided to return to church. Although I'd been trying to convince myself God was not real, the truth was that He was the one calling me back. I knew that my life was getting back on track and that I had to attribute it to him and be thankful for that. There was guilt in my heart because of the extended time I hadn't been to church; I knew it was time to start going again.

Searching for a Baptist church in the South is like searching for sand on a beach. It was logical to look for one close to home, but it wasn't until the third Sunday of my search that I attended Mint Hill Baptist, the church closest to my place.

To this day I don't know why I visited another church that was several miles away. They were great people and were very welcoming. The preaching was very good, and they had programs for people my age. My experience the first two weeks there was excellent, and things were looking up. I had found my church, and I planned to go back the following week.

On the third Sunday, however, my car was as much as parked in the parking lot and I was ready to go in, but that was when I felt a very strong desire to visit the church closest to my house. Pulling out of that parking lot was the beginning of my call to the *páramo*.

Mint Hill Baptist became my new church. It was rare that I missed a Sunday. It was great to be growing again in the things of the Lord. The church had so many ministries, so many opportunities to get involved. Lamar, an elder of the church, introduced himself one day, and our conversation led to an exciting possibility. I shared with him my work on the golf course and how I got to use a lot of Spanish with my coworkers.

Lamar was a tall, mild-mannered man with years of experience that gave him a patience with others I didn't have at the time. His energy was infectious; he had such a youthful enthusiasm that it was a shock to me when he told me he'd been retired for twenty years. His passion for helping others was even more inspiring. He'd been a missionary in Bolivia for several years and wanted to start a Spanish ministry in some communities near the church. He invited me to be part of it. The invitation made perfect sense, because that was exactly where God was moving in my life.

I'd taken a heavy course load in Spanish as well as the sciences. Spanish was always something I enjoyed, and it came easy to me, but there had been very few opportunities to use it where I'd grown up, so I never considered a future in it until I started working on golf courses. The majority of my coworkers did not speak English, so my Spanish was put to good use.

We started the Spanish ministry a few weeks later. It didn't go as smoothly as we'd hoped, but we never stopped giving it our all.

The ministry involved visiting apartment complexes and reaching out to the people there. We would go there on a Saturday afternoon when lots of people were around, and our plan was to connect with some of them and invite them to church.

I was unsure how we would proceed, so I relied on Lamar to see how we would move forward. I'd always assumed that immigrants would adopt an American lifestyle once they got to the States, but that assumption couldn't have been further from the truth; we found pockets in the community where no English was spoken at all.

The main obstacle in our ministry was trying to connect with the people. Lamar was using methods he'd used in Bolivia, including playing music in an open area and inviting listeners to come over and talk. Very few people came over to us, but we tried not to get discouraged. We tried different things over time, but I wasn't much help. I didn't have any methods to offer, and we were working with people from several different countries. It was quite the learning experience.

We eventually learned the effectiveness of one-on-one sharing. We talked with some men in a restaurant; dealing with them in that type of environment made it easier. They opened up to us rather quickly and opened their homes to us shortly after. We became friends with their families and began a Bible study that lasted for a long time after that.

A truth in any kind of ministry, abroad or right at home, is investing in individuals and gaining one disciple at a time. Developing leaders is so effective, and they will grow the ministry. An entire swimming pool can be filled one drop at a time; we just need to be patient. The investment in each person pays enough dividends to fill a thousand swimming pools.

After I'd worked for many weeks with Lamar, an exciting opportunity presented itself. One Sunday after church he shared with me that he had been invited to Venezuela. It's funny, looking back, how things work out. This particular trip to Venezuela was not a mission trip but a reunion for retired missionaries, but Lamar was a man so close to God that he felt there was something for me on this trip anyway. The time was meant for the missionaries to reconnect with former colleagues, but they were planning on doing outreach as well. He told me if I could raise the money to go he would love to have me along. It didn't take much convincing, and I was able to raise the money very quickly. Since I was still living in my uncle's house I wasn't paying rent, so it was easy to save.

At that time I was more intrigued with going to another country than being used by God. I'd been to Canada several years before when our family went to Niagara Falls on vacation. I'd been so focused on my life in North Carolina that I had never thought about getting a passport before, but I got one quickly.

A funny thing happened after Lamar had invited me and before we reached Venezuela. I'd started to pray quite a bit after starting to attend Mint Hill Baptist, but in the short time leading up to our departure I noticed a marked increase in the time I spent in prayer. I was asking God to keep me safe since it would be the first time I'd be on an airplane. That brief request allowed me to spend time with God, just talking to him.

Time always seemed to move slower when I was younger, but the short time of preparation was like a lifetime of learning for me. My mental checklist of things to do before I left was helping me to become better organized. I got everything ready, and two months later we were on our way.

At the time of the invitation I knew Venezuela was somewhere in South America, but I wasn't sure where. I was not familiar with its history nor did I have any clue what the life of a typical Venezuelan person was like. Experiencing this new country firsthand would teach me more than anything I could have learned in geography class anyway. International travel was new to me, but that hadn't stopped Lamar from including me.

Was there anything I'd done or said that had made me stand out to Lamar? I didn't have extensive experience in ministry, nor had I ever studied at a Bible college. I was an average, young professional starting my adult life, and before this my only experience with God had been in the pew on Sunday mornings. I eventually learned that God is worshiped in the pews on Sunday but can be experienced everywhere.

Lamar's shortest missionary journey must have been his walk from the front of the sanctuary to the back pew where I sat. I can't say it was his most effective, but it is one that would impact my life greatly, and for that I am eternally grateful.

Cabimas

Hunched over the counter behind Lamar and several others, I could make out only a bit of the Spanish being spoken around me. Many were asking questions and complaining, wanting to know what was going on. At least the delay was nothing mechanical in nature; the staff at the gate had explained that the plane had just arrived in Miami late. Satisfied by their answer, Lamar bought me a Coke at a deli. We tried to find a place to sit, but there weren't many unoccupied seats.

Long layovers are no fun, but I was too filled with excitement to be annoyed being stuck in Miami due to this delay. Lamar's outgoing nature had us engaged in conversation with all sorts of interesting people. Most of these people were from Venezuela, and speaking with them allowed me to get a quick crash course in the country's culture. The Venezuelans at the gate hadn't met before sitting next to each other at the boarding gate, but it didn't seem that way as their conversation with each other was so lively and familiar.

We finally boarded, and the plane took off. The flight was a smooth one. Sarcastic cheers, typical Venezuelan humor, roared through the cabin as the plane touched down in Maracaibo an hour late.

My first memory of Venezuela was that of a dimly lit runway and a long walk outside from the plane to the terminal. Even late at night it was incredibly warm. A bus was waiting for us as we exited the terminal, and a few minutes later we left the airport. As we made our way to the hotel, I remember the excitement of seeing billboards in Spanish and salsa music playing on the bus at full volume. The front door of the bus was wide open, and a warm breeze came in as we went down the highway.

We finally got to the hotel on the north side of Maracaibo. The lobby was surprisingly modern, and the front desk staff spoke very good English. The cold from the air conditioning was such a relief from the humid, warm air outside. Things felt very different yet strangely familiar. We were so tired when we finally reached our room we went to sleep immediately. A brief planning meeting followed by a devotional and prayer time was to start early in the morning anyway, so we needed our rest.

We arrived at the meeting the next morning and had a breakfast typical of those back home: eggs, toast, and orange juice. Though I was by far the youngest in the group, I felt included in all the activities, which eased my original feelings of discomfort.

My eyes scanned the group, and I took in my surroundings. An image still burned into my memory is of a missionary serving in Venezuela at the time in tears as these other missionaries began to sing worship songs in Spanish. It was a moving time, but it is only now that I can fully appreciate the emotion he was feeling at that moment, a flood of thanksgiving to God for his call to that place.

Then came the change of plans that changed the course of my life. After catching up, these missionaries had planned on venturing out to help different churches. We were planning on staying right in Maracaibo. An American missionary who worked in that region approached us with the news of a church in Cabimas, about forty-five minutes away, that was struggling to grow. Being sent there ended up being another confirmation of my call, another step toward the paramo.

Cabimas, a small city on the east coast of Lake Maracaibo, is home for the many petroleum workers who work on the lake. The church we would eventually be sent to, as the American missionary explained, had been around for many years but was going through some very tough times. The church board had hired a pastor who had led the congregation astray. This particular pastor had brought in a doctrine (or teaching) much different from the Baptist Church and even threatened to break the church away from the Baptist Convention, a decision which would have put the ownership of the building in question. The decision cost them not only a majority of their members but very nearly the building they worshiped in.

We left the next day to meet the newly installed missionary in Cabimas and to offer our services for the week. Our trip that day took us across the General Rafael Urdaneta Bridge, which spans the narrowest part of Lake Maracaibo and connects the north of Zulia State with the mainland of Venezuela.

Known affectionately in Venezuela as El Puente (the bridge), it has had songs and poems written about it and is the longest concrete span bridge in Latin America. The trip across was exciting, but that day I was so wrapped up in the task ahead of us I didn't even notice that we'd driven on the bridge for five and a half miles. I relish these facts now as I have crossed this bridge over one hundred times since.

The ride from Maracaibo to Cabimas isn't very far, and as we reached the other side of the lake we still seemed to be in a very urban environment. The east coast of the lake was fairly well developed with many businesses, restaurants, and homes. Occasionally we'd pass an undeveloped patch of land and get a clear view of the beautiful lake and many boats on the water. As we neared Cabimas, the brief views we got of the water revealed the oil rigs in Lake Maracaibo. We started to see large, off-shore pumps nestled between homes and streets. These were neat to see; I had no idea this country produced so much oil!

Though Cabimas is much smaller than Maracaibo, it is still considered a city. As we took some side streets on the way to the church, we began to see houses with tin roofs, unpaved streets, and mangy animals walking about. We were still in a large city, but it seemed that we'd gone back in time.

Our driver dropped us off at the front door of the church. The missionary pastor, Guillermo, a short man with glasses, a round face, and a permanent smile, made me comfortable right away. I could tell I was with a pastor from his deep love for people, and his lighthearted nature and constant jokes took away the uneasy feeling that came with meeting people. Many times before, when talking with pastors, I felt a need to guard myself in order to refrain from talking about my past. With Guillermo that wasn't necessary. He just loved the Lord and loved people, and much like Jesus, he met them where they were.

As a missionary with the Venezuelan Baptist Convention, Guillermo had been sent to Cabimas a few weeks previously to rescue this church from ruin. Just a remnant of its members was left. We worked with this group and went out every day to visit and invite people to services we were to have each night. I learned very quickly that even though I'd been in their country for only three days, Venezuelans consider anyone who comes to help them minister a missionary. I was introduced to the community and even in church services as such and just got used to it.

At one point Guillermo thrust me behind the pulpit to preach. My sermons lasted all of five minutes and were delivered in nervous, broken Spanish but were still received with hearty *Amens!* from the enthusiastic congregation. I learned to be ready at all times for God to use you regardless of your title, but back then, in my mind I was no more a missionary than Kareem Abdul-Jabar was an airplane pilot. The church leaders didn't seem to see it that way. My past, my lost years at college, and the appearances I tried to keep didn't matter. In my mind I was going to be a tourist for ten days and head home, back to the golf course, to the life I loved. I could go all in with this missionary idea or just sit on the sidelines counting the days until it was over. But I soon found that I hadn't landed in Venezuela by chance and that God was going to use me however he was going to use me. I had a choice to make. I decided to make the most of it.

I made lifelong friends on that trip. When the week was over, Guillermo laid out his five-year plan for his congregation and wanted me to be part of it. After the ten days with him I had no choice but to believe him when he said God was calling me to be a missionary. I didn't make any immediate commitments, but there was too much peace in my heart for me to believe that it was nonsense. The greatest lesson I'd learned to that point was that the confirmation of a call is always accompanied by peace.

An Important Decision

After Guillermo's invitation, I returned to Charlotte quite different from when I had left. Our conversation was stuck in my mind, and I couldn't get it out. The whole time I contemplated possibilities, the peace about future decisions never left my heart.

In my youth I'd been on fascinating vacations with my family, so I couldn't attribute my feelings completely to the euphoria one feels after returning from an exciting trip to a faraway place. And I was anxious to get back to work at the golf course; it wasn't in my plans to leave that behind just yet.

At work, I spent a lot of time on a tractor mowing fairways and greens; the hours of solitude gave me time to think. More and more I was thinking about Cabimas, Guillermo, the church, and its youth group. My thoughts were focused on people, not just experiences, so it felt God himself was putting these thoughts in my mind.

Riding a mower morning after morning, I thought about the people who Guillermo and I had visited. I thought about their dirt floors in their cramped houses and about their gracious hospitality. These families had opened their doors to a complete stranger like me without any hesitation.

The thought of the kids in the church's community was what most prevailed in my mind. One day Guillermo and I had been walking through the streets looking for kids to invite to church. The kids were playing *flichita*, street baseball played with broomsticks and bottle caps. One kid yelled, "I'll go to church if he can hit one."

He was referring to me.

I must have swung and missed at a hundred pitches, and then I connected. The bottle cap sailed over everyone's head and into the living room of the house across the street. Guillermo started laughing, and all the kids started cheering. We saw two or three of them at church the last Sunday we were there. These would be the kids I'd be working with if I returned to work with Guillermo. It took a few months of prayer and reflection, but I finally decided to go back to Cabimas to work with the church.

The following summer I returned to Cabimas to work with the church for two years, and there was so much to be done. A volunteer team from Mint Hill Baptist accompanied me to Cabimas and stayed for a week. This team, just like I had done on my first trip to Cabimas, had come during the week of their Vacation Bible School with plans of helping. No one from the group spoke Spanish, so they were relying on me to be their interpreter as well.

It was nice to see a commitment to missions from our home church. I was going to be working as a missions intern with the International Missions Board. Guillermo had sent a request to them for me to work with him. The good news was that I was accepted into the program. The bad news was that they felt needs were more urgent in Caracas, twelve hours by bus, and the board planned to send me there to work.

I was able to accompany the volunteer team for the week before leaving for Caracas. We had a great experience. We took part in the Vacation Bible School for neighborhood children that went well. Members from other Baptist churches in Cabimas came to help us, and it helped us form relationships with them. We were even invited to share a few times with them during the week.

This working relationship has lasted throughout the years, making Cabimas a very special place for me. It is good to have brothers and sisters from many churches to share with and visit when I'm able. On my first trip there I needed to be escorted everywhere. Now I know all the *porpuesto,* or taxi, routes and even know some great shortcuts to get to Maracaibo a bit quicker.

Guillermo was also sharing with us about La Puerta, a town about three hours away to which he'd travel two days a week. It was not possible for me to visit that town as I was getting things ready for my move to Caracas. A few team members went there for a day but didn't say much about it. I wasn't sure if I would ever visit that town, but I found out a few months later that God was there, waiting for me.

Just as we were starting to feel at home in Cabimas it was time to leave. The church had a special good-bye service for us. It's never easy to say good-bye even when you feel you may see someone again. My good-bye was twice as hard because I was splitting from my new friends in Cabimas and also from my Mint Hill Baptist Church brothers and sisters who were heading home. My two-year internship would be starting, and I was off to Caracas.

CHAPTER 5

New Life in Distrito Federal

My flight from Maracaibo to Caracas was quick, and just like that I was alone.

Every moment I'd previously spent in this country I'd been with someone at my side, but from that point on I was left to find my way without the guidance of friends or colleagues. Making my way off the plane, I clutched the strap of my backpack tightly as a feeling of unease began to overtake me. After a few minutes my bags popped off the conveyor and started making their way to me. I grabbed them and walked toward the scanner. The light blinked green, my things made it through security, and I was good to go, so I proceeded toward the exit.

Immediately I was swarmed by people trying to help me with my bags. Some were extremely pushy, but I refused to let them touch anything. All I heard around me was a slurred buzz of Spanish. Alone in a city of millions, I tried to figure out where my new supervisor was and what he looked like.

I saw children jumping up and down as they awaited their loved ones. Adults too were waving and shouting as family and friends came out. I saw taxi drivers carrying signs bearing people's names, and I hoped to see my new supervisor with a big sign that read "Bienvenido Mateo!" or something of the sort. I saw no such sign. The experience started to become more stressful than fun.

It turned out that because most new missionaries arrived on international rather than domestic flights, my supervisor and his family were waiting for me at the international terminal, next door. We never met up at the airport, and I was left to make it into the city by myself.

In a city of millions without my supervisor's address or phone number to rely on, I learned another lesson: when you step out in faith to serve God, there will be struggles. A major roadblock already, and it was just day one. How would God get me through this one? The assumption is that things always work out fine for missionaries since they're on God's side. The truth is that there are plenty of struggles that try us, but God will eventually get us through them.

I found a taxi driver willing to drive me to Caracas, forty-five minutes from the airport. But taxis in Venezuela are not like those in New York. The drivers basically make up their own fares. They jump at the chance to take advantage of you. It was nothing like the loving Venezuela I'd experienced previously. What had I gotten myself into with this two-year commitment?

Back in Cabimas I'd been given the address of a friend of a friend of a friend. I was also given clear instructions to not hesitate at all to bother complete strangers if I needed anything. This is customary in Venezuelan culture, but I didn't think I'd need to cash in so quickly on this favor, or ever for that matter. The driver dropped me off at that address and tried charging me three times the normal fare. With the help of this complete stranger at the house who became a quick friend, we talked him down to accepting just twice the normal fare. And so my stay in Caracas began.

The missionary who was to be my supervisor for a few weeks until Richard (eventually my regular supervisor) got back from furlough was able to locate me by e-mail, and a few hours later he was at the door to pick me up. We drove to my new apartment, which was large and incredibly secure. It had an outside gate with a lock, an outer *reja,* or barred door, and a heavy wooden door with a bolt. Would these doors ever be kept open? It seemed that Caracas was a bit dangerous, but even if the bars and deadbolts weren't enough, I'd still have the hands of God to protect me.

It was late when we finally got in, so we didn't talk much; I went right to bed. The next morning we conversed at length, and I will never forget what he said. "Matthew, we expect your next few years to be the best years of your life." I didn't respond but thought *Would it be possible to be as happy and fulfilled as when I was in Charlotte?* I wasn't sure what to think. Put another tally in God's column; He blessed me and changed me during those years in a way I still can't believe.

Justin, another missions intern, was the Caracas host for the mission board. He also made trips to the airport to receive new missionaries. Justin had responsibilities outside of Caracas that day and could not make it. That was a shame, because he turned out to be an example of what a servant should be, and if I had met him that day my two years may have gotten off to a better start. He was always there to help us when we needed him, and we eventually became good friends.

Caracas, Venezuela's capital, is known as the *distrito federal,* the federal district. Many just say D.F. when referring to it. My assignment was to work with the city's university students. I had the full backing of the mission board in this effort, but as a pioneer in this outreach it was up to me alone to start the work. Other missionaries my age were there, working in other areas and willing to show me around the city and teach me the bus routes and the subway system.

Caracas, a very large city, has a main artery that is always somehow affected by gridlock. The city is not a modern one; it is a throwback to the architectural styles of the early nineteen eighties. There are huge skyscrapers, just like in any large U.S. city, but they are shaped much differently and seem to be scattered about, without any sort of order. Their colors are all a faded gray and have a worn appearance to them. It is evident when you see them that you are in a foreign country. The deafening sounds and smells of the many buses running to and fro filled the air, and there always seemed to be someone shouting or blowing a whistle somewhere. Every bus that traverses the city is jam-packed with humanity of all walks, from a mother taking her child to the park and an elderly person going for groceries to an urban professional trying to make it across the city to work. The *colectores*, the fare collectors, shout for more passengers as they hang out the front of the bus with one arm.

It didn't take long for me to learn that the main point of orientation in Caracas is El Avila mountain that separates Caracas from the Caribbean and helped you find your way in the city. Once you located north on your mental compass by finding El Avila, you could usually figure out where you were going. I spent many a fun and interesting day up there hiking and exploring.

For the most part, the city runs from east to west behind Avila, and the main *autopista*, or highway, runs parallel to it, as does the main subway line, which has two minor branches that run south from two main points in the city. A majority of the city can be reached by subway, but parts are accessible only by bus.

It took about three days until I was up to venturing out on my own. I learned some key subway stations and became able to meet people in certain places without getting lost. I heard a funny story about a missionary new to Caracas who was to meet someone at a subway restaurant. Evidently she didn't realize that the underground network of trains in the city was not called the subway, because she was waiting for them at the entrance to the subway while the other party waited in the restaurant by that name; the city's subway system is called the metro.

The good thing was that the main university had its own subway stop, and I could make it there on my own, but it was always good to have someone with me. Kevin, another missions intern working in our business office, was familiar with the city and offered to show me one of its universities. Though Caracas is home to over fifty universities and colleges, I ended up working in just four.

That first day Kevin took me to the Universidad Central de Venezuela (UCV), the country's largest university, which enrolls students from every part of Venezuela and offers majors in several disciplines, including law, medicine, and business from undergraduate to doctorate levels. The two options where I felt I could relate even remotely with students for my first visit were the school of science or the modern language department. Fortunately Kevin had already made some friends in the school of modern languages.

One of the splendid things about the universities in Venezuela was the amount of outdoor cafés. Kevin had arranged a meeting with some of his friends at one of the cafés at the language school. I remember being so nervous, as if I were going to a job interview. I had no idea what to expect. But when God goes before us, we are assured victorious results. Our meeting went better than good. In fact, we met four students that day, and they all continued to meet with me in the English conversation club. One of them, Erica, is one of my closest friends to this day.

As the students and I conversed and got to know each other, they shared information about their language program. UCV language students study two foreign languages simultaneously. The students meeting with us that day were all studying English, so though our conversation started out in Spanish, they were excited to have two *gringos* at their disposal and began to ask us questions about American slang.

We were happy to oblige; it was so much fun to see their faces each time they learned a new American term. Their English was excellent, and I was thoroughly impressed. All they had to do was reduce their accents and learn some slang to be able to join a conversation of native English speakers without missing a beat.

Including my two visits to Cabimas, I'd been in Venezuela a grand total of three weeks at that point but had not yet had a Venezuelan coffee. I had no idea what I was ordering; Kevin did that for me. The only coffee you could get was espresso, which is prepared a number of ways. My limited coffee drinking experience left me clueless. I remember my first sip, powerful but exquisite. My memory will always bring me back to that first coffee, the beginning of a lifelong love affair.

We left our meeting that day with plans to form an English conversation club. We planned to meet one day a week with that group of four. A few weeks later I noticed advertisements for the club around the language department and a growing number in our group each week. The growing group had to be divided, and I began meeting three times a week with different groups. The groups were very informal, and the topics of conversation ranged from sports and politics to music and even world religions.

Meeting in small, informal groups with the students allowed us to connect on a really personal level. We began spending time outside the university, which helped me expand my knowledge of the city and its sites of interest. Mondays in Venezuela were half-price movie nights at all theaters in country, and we made it a tradition to go. Visits to shopping malls and burger joints were more and more frequent as time went on. Venezuelan food was a delight, and my friends were teaching me a lot about that too.

I had my first *arepa*, a doughnut-shaped cylinder made from corn meal, in Cabimas, but I won't forget the first one I had in Caracas. Arepas, the staple of the Venezuelan diet, are sometimes fried but generally grilled; people have them for breakfast, lunch, and even dinner when the mood strikes. They can accompany a meal or be the meal themselves. They can simply be cut open and buttered, just like bread, as was the case with the first one I had in Cabimas, but Venezuelans can be very creative when it comes to what to fill them with besides butter. At many street food stands I'd see arepas filled with everything from pork chops to macaroni salad. My first Caracas arepa was filled with pieces of hot dog mixed with mayonnaise. Venezuelan culture was basically the same all over the country, but its culture had variations from city to city. That variation, along with the arepas, was something I liked a lot about living there.

My students were teaching me so much, and I enjoyed our growing friendships. I prayed for my students every day. I was sent there to share Jesus with them, but I was also getting to know them. They were becoming more special to me every day. Their friendship was a treasure, something I valued. Simply preaching to them would alienate them and give them the impression that their "conversion" was my only interest. As I prayed for them, their families, and their safety, God gave me wisdom and insight.

I wanted to put God first in everything, but doing so I didn't want to push people to the side. God comes before all things, but people aren't absent from that equation. All people are important to God, those who attend church and those who don't. The revelation that God showed me through those times of prayer was just that.

Getting to know these students allowed me to get to know their personal needs. Meeting people's needs is far more important than simply preaching to them. The Bible tells us to always be sharing God's truth, but Christian pretense is a horrible thing. We can't just throw Bible verses at people so we can feel good about ourselves and then abandon them and move on. Meeting needs is important.

These students had become special to me as they were to him. Sharing God's truth with them was only slightly more important than getting to know them. Although God should be above all things, the way we treat people and seek to know them intimately is vital. The mistake we make a lot is forgetting that he is already there working in their hearts.

When I think of the time I spent with Lamar, I remember what I learned from him, the importance of investing in people. In a city of millions, my scope of influence was limited to around ten. But their mere number did not make them insignificant, and I found that even with a limited number, more of God's love could be concentrated and focused just on them.

This was all new to me, with such a limited experience in ministry. During our meetings the students started asking me questions about the Bible I couldn't answer. It forced me to rely more on God in prayer and study of his Word. Answers were never lacking for these seekers. They may not have come in the moment the questions were asked, but they did come.

Investing in these students allowed me to get to know their strengths, their weaknesses, their passions, and their talents. It also allowed me to encourage them and help them make good decisions in life. I thought of all the bad decisions I'd made before then because no one had encouraged me in times of decision making. Learning about God along with my students was a surreal experience.

Another lesson I learned was that the infinite nature of God never allows us to stop learning more about him. Regardless of your past, regardless of what you would consider adequate preparation, God wants to use you. We should always strive to learn and prepare ourselves, but it is a journey.

A disciple is one who embraces and assists in the teachings of another. The key word here is "embraces." I'm a disciple of

Christ because I choose to be, not because anyone is forcing me. Many nonbelievers think that what we do as Christians is indoctrinate. That could not be further from the truth. Jesus says to his disciples that "By this shall all men know that ye are my disciples, if ye have love one to another." Here he stresses love, which comes before knowledge and leads us to knowledge. We get this backward so many times, and our ministries suffer as a result.

During this process of adapting to missionary life, I was presenting God's truth to these students. Many were curious at first but stopped seeking after a while. They were people in whom I had invested time, but they weren't disciples. They were interested in the things of God for a while but made the decision to continue solely as English students. Our relationship did not change as a result even though they didn't embrace the spiritual truths offered them.

I always had an idea that missionaries were supposed to have multitudes of disciples and "missions" established. We don't control our results; we can control only our obedience. Of all the university students I shared with, very few disciples resulted, but I certainly remember my first true disciple and how we met.

My Esteemed Friend

Pastor Xergio had told me to meet him at the BP gas station in Santa Fe at 6:00 p.m. This was a section of Caracas that was a very short bus ride away, so I arrived early. At 6:45 he had not yet arrived. Knowing that traffic in the city is ridiculously bad at all hours of the day, I continued to wait. Venezuelans are not particularly punctual, but I was getting impatient. I began pacing.

The sky grew dark, as the sun set around 6:30 throughout the year. A few minutes later Pastor Xergio showed up almost as if he were early. We drove a few blocks and parked the car. The dinner was supposed to start at seven, and we got there just in time.

Xergio and I are roughly the same age. His excellent English and sense of humor helped us grow close right away. He is a pastor of a small congregation in the city and has helped me connect with different churches reaching out to university students.

The Mission Board backed me in my efforts with the university students and helped in connecting me with pastors and university outreaches throughout the city and country. That night we were meeting a group of Christian university students led by a Korean pastor who met with them regularly for fellowship. I'd been invited by Xergio to share with them at a dinner meeting.

When we walked in many were still mingling. Xergio introduced me to the pastor who had organized this activity. We talked for a while and went to eat. We were seated near Brigitte, an English student studying at a teachers' college in the city. We got acquainted over dinner. We spoke in Spanish, and Xergio giggled at my choice of words. Some of the Spanish words I still use do not match the Venezuelan lexicon, and even close friends were amused at my strange vocabulary at times. Brigitte and I discussed the possibility of my visiting her school to start an English group. She was preparing to be an English teacher and had several classmates who were interested in improving their English.

I asked Brigitte questions about this teachers' institute; it looked as though this would be an opportunity to share with another group of English students. We continued to talk, even after dinner, and the contrast in size between her school, El Instituto Pedagogico de Caracas, a teachers' institute, and other schools around Caracas became evident. I explained to her that I was working only at UCV, the largest university in the country, more than twice the size of her college, the Ped, as it was affectionately known.

Brigitte was a bit shy and reserved. I could tell she was hoping I could find the time to meet her classmates although she never said anything. I asked if I could visit the Ped the following week, and she said it seemed like a good idea.

The trip there required two bus rides, a subway ride, and a five-block walk through a section of town crowded with street vendors and salsa music playing at full volume. The trip was a small price to pay for the blessing that awaited me there. Doors open up everywhere in life, and we have to be aware of them being open to be able to walk through them. The opportunity at the Ped was a good one. The school was smaller, but the desire of the students to learn English was great. Given the size of the school few outsiders came to help them, so my being there added to their enthusiasm. My schedule allowed me two days with them, and we hit the ground running.

It was up to me to find the school's English department. I had to ask directions a few times, but it wasn't long before I found the fourth floor of the humanities building. It was just after 1:00 p.m., and Brigitte had told me she'd be in class until 2:00.

I sat in a small lounge behind a stairwell and was able to see everyone coming and going. I greeted students as they passed, and they all seemed very friendly. After an hour I spied Brigitte and ran to greet her. She was so surprised to see me. "I have an important meeting at the church," she said, "But I have a few minutes to introduce you to some classmates."

I followed her down a hallway to a classroom. She motioned inside, and a girl came out. "Mateo, this is Dagmar," said Brigitte in the way of introduction.

"Nice to meet you, Dagmar," I said. "You seem to be busy right now. Can I wait until your class is over so we can talk?" Dagmar agreed. Brigitte was in a hurry to go, so she asked me if I would be all right waiting by myself. I thanked her and told her that I'd be fine. She expressed interest in knowing how my meeting with Dagmar went, so I agreed to call her later.

An hour hadn't passed before Dagmar walked up. I hadn't noticed how short she was. I felt as if I were with an old friend, though she was yet to smile. As we talked, I noticed she had a very businesslike manner. She said that she and a majority of her classmates wanted to improve their English by practicing with a native speaker.

Dagmar may have thought she was talking to a tenured professor considering the notes she took and her questions about what level students I normally worked with. I told her that I was there simply to offer my services and that the students' level of English was not that important.

It was then I heard her wonderful chuckle for the first time. "Oh, okay, okay," she laughed as she spoke, now understanding that the group would be more like a club than a class. "We could meet on Tuesdays right after lunch if you can make it then," she said. "Everyone who would be interested in this group has class on Tuesday mornings, and most of us are free after lunch." We happened to be talking on a Monday, so I was back the next day to get started with the English conversation club.

Our group was small to start out, but it allowed us to share a lot of grammar and slang. They quickly learned that Americans did not literally "let the cat of the bag," or "sleep with one eye open." Some American expressions had them laughing for complete ninety-minute sessions. Experiences like these taught me to appreciate the Venezuelan sense of humor. My expectation had been that Venezuelans would be more serious, but that was not true, and I saw that firsthand as I spent time with my new friends.

Dagmar was a key member of this group from the start. She was the one who had put the group together, and it was clear she had amazing leadership skills. Her English was good, and I could tell she would have great success as a teacher. Our sessions at the Ped were more formal, more like classes. We shared a lot of reading material, everything from *The New York Times* to various magazine articles and even classic novels.

One day in a meeting with my supervisor, we found that a group from the States had sent a box of English Bibles for us to use. The group at the Ped enjoyed reading in English quite a bit, so I brought a few to our next session. I felt I would ask first if they would be offended by receiving a Bible as a gift, and they told me I was crazy for thinking that (Dagmar chuckled after she called me crazy).

Immediately our time was dominated by studying Bible passages. Questions were asked not just about the Old English style and wording of the King James Version but also about the truths contained in them. They were embracing these truths and wanted to learn more. Our time was supposed to be utilized practicing English, but I could tell when their curiosity about the things of God was sparked.

Their questions started coming in Spanish, the language of their hearts. It wasn't just a superficial curiosity; it was a deep longing to know more. This longing is inside every human being, though many try to deny it's there. God himself was using me to knock on the door of their hearts, and they were responding. Dagmar prayed a prayer with me shortly after to accept Christ as her personal Savior. She was my first disciple; she truly embraced the truths shared with her and wanted to know more.

Dagmar and I had little in common at first, but we grew close anyway. The bond that kept us growing closer was the time of Bible study we shared. I had two sisters back in the States, but Dagmar quickly became the sister I needed there. She looked out for me and gave me great tips on staying safe in Caracas. She shared some stories about what had happened to friends of hers, native Venezuelans, and how a few minutes of letting their guard down led to a robbery. These stories helped me to be more aware of my surrounding while traveling throughout Caracas. She also taught me the trick I still use today, to carry my cash and credit cards in my front pocket and to leave my wallet at home. When my mother and two sisters visited me in Venezuela, we had lunch with Dagmar. It was like a family reunion even though she'd just met them.

Of all the people I had the privilege of knowing in Venezuela, Dagmar will always have a special place in my heart. Even now I visit her in Caracas and we go to her nieces' dance recitals, family picnics, and other activities. If she is not one of the first people I call on the phone upon arriving in Venezuela, she doesn't let me hear the end of it. But there's never any reason for me not to call her right away; she means the world to me.

I was an English teacher for my students, but being there serving as a missionary gave it another dimension. Not only did I get to know the people very well, but I became one of them. I'm glad to have been welcomed as part of Dagmar's family too.

A custom in Venezuela is for sons, daughters, nieces, and nephews to ask for a blessing from family elders. Dagmar is now married and has a little boy. I remember Dagmar putting his hands together when he was a baby in a patty-cake motion and speaking for him. "Bendicion Tio Mateo," she said. "Bless me, Uncle Matt." This was a rite of passage for me and her way of telling me I was not only her friend but also part of her intimate family circle.

Many students and friends have touched my life in a special way in Venezuela. I remember them all with affection and thanksgiving. I call Dagmar my esteemed friend. She was the first disciple I ever had in Venezuela. Meeting her not only changed the course of my remaining time in Caracas, but it changed the direction of my ministry forever.

CHAPTER 7

A Permanent Visitor

Our mission board was in Venezuela as a partner to its National Baptist Convention. In addition to our commitment to our individual ministries, we were also invited to national conferences from time to time. I was not in the country too long before we were all invited to Maracaibo to meet with Venezuelan pastors and missionaries from the Venezuelan National Baptist Convention. At that time Richard was my supervisor, and he suggested I go to meet pastors around the country and be formally presented to the convention.

The only other time I had traveled a distance that great in Venezuela was when I flew from Maracaibo to Caracas. The nine-hour car trip from Caracas to Maracaibo was my first taste of Venezuelan highways. Counting landmarks made the trip more bearable. Highway travel in Venezuela is a bit slower and can be dangerous. Gas stations around the country are full service. Richard would pull up to the pump and just say "Full." He spoke this English word with a Spanish accent, but I found it humorous that even a simple English word was understood by the workers.

We passed through a desert, an area that gets only a few inches of rain a year. At least this section of the trip was flat and straight. Barquisimeto is the largest city in the desert, but even when we got there after five hours of driving we were just a little over halfway.

The rest of the trip seemed to have no end until we finally came to the bridge that spans Lake Maracaibo. Richard may have been getting tired of hearing my stories about Cabimas as we started to see some exits for it just before crossing the bridge. We made it to the other side of the lake, and I was back in Maracaibo, which felt pretty good.

On the first day of the assembly I was seated next to Robert, one of our short-term missionaries. He suddenly had a look of shock and happiness on his face as the then–presidential candidate and governor of Zulia State, Francisco Arias Cardenas, shook our hands on his way to the podium. His speech was more political than spiritual, but it was awesome to be witnessing a speech from a nationally recognized leader.

On the last day of the assembly we were approached by Pastor Botto and his son, Enoch. They were from a small church in San Carlos del Zulia, a town about four hours from Maracaibo, on the southern end of the lake. They introduced themselves during a recess a few minutes after I was presented to the assembly as a new missionary.

The father and son approached me and participated in a custom that most here keep; they invited me to their church to share our university ministry with them, and they also invited themselves to Caracas to visit me. I wasn't sure if I would ever see them again, but it was nice to meet them. Enoch and his father were both very friendly and seemed genuinely interested in our university work. After speaking with them for a few minutes, my supervisor tapped me on the shoulder to let me know we were leaving soon. It was the third and last day of the assembly.

We left the heat of Maracaibo and stopped for the night in Valencia, about two hours past Barquisimeto. Richard introduced me to another missionary who had also put in a request for me to work with him with university students here. The two had business unrelated to me and to the university work, but it was nice to break up our return trip.

After Valencia, a series of curves and tunnels takes you through the mountains that protect the capital city. I always forget to count the tunnels and curves, and to this day I always forget a few when traveling east toward Caracas because many look the same.

Kids and adults circle your car at one particular tollbooth to sell fresh cheese from the plains of Venezuela, some of the best I have ever had in my life. We rarely ever buy it here, but we used this specific toll as a landmark that told us we were about an hour from Caracas.

Having left Valencia at an early hour and having a short drive, we arrived in Caracas, avoiding rush hour thanks to Richard's timing. We were refreshed and ready to go back to work. I didn't have any appointments that day, so I hung out at UCV, where I always went when I didn't have other plans. The next day my regular schedule returned and life was back to normal—but it was never dull.

A few weeks after returning from the meeting in Maracaibo, Enoch called to say he would be in Caracas to file paperwork there for the church and asked if he could stay for a few days. He arrived a few days later to complete his errands.

Enoch used the guest bedroom in the apartment I shared with another intern, but he had to wait for us to let him in every night because he didn't have a key, as we thought he would be staying only a few days. We waited for him every night with looks of concern on our faces. He was in his native country, but Caracas can be dangerous, so we felt better when he made it back safely each night.

A two-day visit to complete some errands turned into a few weeks. Enoch started to accompany us to the grocery store, which may have been a clue that he had no plans on leaving. He stayed as a guest in our home for the next two years, an important adjustment I had to make to be a good host to my guest and grow a healthy working relationship with him, a partner in ministry. Once the students got to know him, they found he had a wonderful sense of humor and a contagious laugh. He wasn't at all athletic, but he kept up with me on my rigorous trips to the universities, where I had to walk several blocks in a very short period of time. Enoch was a great help to me, visiting in the universities and organizing activities. His lengthy visit was an unexpected one, but he immediately made himself an asset to our university team and became a very good friend to all of us.

CHAPTER 8

A Glimpse into Our Future

In an unexpectedly quiet section of Caracas Kevin and I sat at an outdoor café with some of our English students. We were conversing about various topics, mostly in English and occasionally in Spanish. Kevin had been coming for a while at that point and had invited us to enjoy a night of relaxation and conversation. "My visa is expiring soon," I told Kevin, taking advantage of the brief moments that we were alone while the others had gone to order. I continued, "They will probably send me to Aruba. I could deal with that I guess."

It was another great Caracas evening, evidence of why it's known as the City of Eternal Spring with a year 'round mild climate. The low lighting on the patio and the still air made us forget quickly we were outside. The music playing gently in the background was an eclectic mix of salsa music, soft rock, and jazz.

Kevin had been very good friends with Pastor Xergio and had told me that he was coming that night. Very few young people attended Pastor Xergio's church, so he liked to help us reach out to students. We were hoping to see him walking up to the café, but in the meantime Kevin and I continued our conversation about renewing our visas.

"I actually wanted to see if you'd take a trip to Peru with me," Kevin replied. By then the students were heading back to the table, so the English exchange with our students resumed. I participated in the dialogue but was thinking about the possibility Kevin had just presented.

In order to renew our six-month visas we had to leave the country for at least twenty-four hours, so it was a good opportunity to take a vacation. We began planning just a few days after Kevin mentioned the trip. Because we'd be traveling during the off-peak season, airfare was very reasonable. Kevin and I discussed the proper attire for hiking and made sure we had warm, rugged clothes that would protect us from the elements. After several weeks of waiting and planning, Justin did us the favor of taking us to the airport, and Kevin and I flew to Lima and from there to Cusco.

At Cusco, just below the ancient site of Machu Picchu, we decided to take a three-day hike to the site rather than a one-hour bus ride. Our tour group consisted of a guide, who spoke six languages, and some natives to the area who carried our supplies and ran ahead to set up any one night's camp. Traveling with us for those three days were also a newlywed couple from Germany and two friends from Chile who were here hiking this trail for the second time. We got to know each other well and shared many stories over the campfire each night.

The sights were remarkable. Our orientation took place at the foot of the mountain on a small patch of flat land sandwiched between two towering mountains. I was wondering if a trail went between them or if we were going to walk straight up one of them. Long, puffy clouds were abbreviated by the towering mountains, but there was a little bit of space left over for some blue skies to show through. We were ready to explore this wonderful place, a unique experience.

We were soon thankful for the help carrying our supplies. Kevin and I were both in the prime of our lives, in excellent physical shape. I was an avid swimmer and was even practicing with a water polo team in Caracas. This hike wouldn't nearly compare to the rigorous training water polo requires, or so I thought. This hike would be a piece of cake. It looked so easy for the men running with our tents and bags of food; they literally ran ahead of us and made it look so easy. Even working out as much as I did, I quickly realized there was no way I could ever do that.

A good bit of the hike resembled a casual, enjoyable stroll since we weren't carrying much weight. Our guide explained the history of the place at different points along the way. Most of our trek was through a protected valley, but we were treated to breathtaking views after a significant climb.

At one point in the hike, at about sixteen thousand feet, steps led to the highest point on the hike, a distance measuring a few hundred feet. With each step I was going slower; the thin air was wearing on me. It took us close to two hours to reach the top of the stairs. The humbling part was seeing the men running past us with pounds of weight on their backs. We were slow to adapt to these surroundings. We thought we could handle it, but we were not ready. The good thing was that there was someone else more suited for the task.

The climb made us weary, but we could see for miles from the top. The day was a bit overcast, but we were still able to see the mountain peaks in the distance, one folded behind the other. We wanted to stay there all day, but after a few minutes of rest our guide had us going again. A short downhill walk brought us to our night's camp.

It was so much fun to camp out and spend time around the fire with our tour group, enjoying the night sky and the crisp air. There were travelers from as far away as Germany hiking with us. The Andes were a spectacular site. I'd hiked in New York's Catskills, but in Machu Picchu we scaled peaks two to three times higher. If the sites alone weren't enough, what we learned from our guide about Incan culture was fascinating. I was overcome by intrigue and emotion.

We finally reached Machu Picchu after a long three days. There is no way we could ever forget what we saw that day, seeing it get closer and closer with every bend in the trail. The final stretch of the path gave us a clear view of the ruins. This was not a postcard; we were actually there!

We could see layer upon layer of ruins. I was at a loss for words, having all this in my sights at last. The site was so much bigger than I had expected. This city was divided like any other would be. It appeared to have residential and industrial sections. The grass was so green, and it wasn't hard imagining how they kept it cut short years ago; judging by the ruins, they did everything with extraordinary efficiency.

We began to merge with busloads of tourists who would be touring the grounds with us that day. Some Asian tourists were listening to tour presentations on headphones, further heightening the magnitude of this experience.

The ruins were incredible. The structures had been built by hand and had stood for centuries. The worn surfaces of the stones were evidence of the history of this place. Each structure was in a perfectly engineered position to fulfill its function.

Our guide said good-bye at that point and headed down the mountain. Kevin and I had the option of hooking up with some other groups who were starting their tour, but we decided to explore the grounds ourselves.

Kevin and I learned the importance of a guide, a helper, and a friend as we hiked. We knew that there would come times when we felt weak and stagnant and that those three elements would be necessary. Just like the Inca trail we'd hiked, we come to places in our lives where we feel overwhelmed and impotent.

We took this knowledge with us as we went from this place. God showed me the three elements on that hike. We had a guide who had shown us where to go and taught us about different landmarks and about the history of certain artifacts. Kevin and I referred to a book about Machu Picchu often during our hike, and our guide explained everything, bringing even the smallest detail to life. It is always good to have someone to guide us in wisdom and truth.

On that steep staircase, at so high an elevation, we needed someone to help us carry the weight. Those helpers were carrying our tents and food, the trip would have been impossible without them. We always need someone who has walked in our shoes and can carry the burden for us when we can't and to do so whenever we need it.

Friends are important. At those high elevations and in the cold, Kevin and I were together, motivating each other. The encouragement was great, and it was so good to have someone to share the wonderful experience with.

I never regretted the decision to go to Machu Picchu, an awesome experience. Sometimes we think our destiny depends solely on the decisions we make, but there are times we see the hand of God directing us. I went back a few months later with the intention of visiting Machu Picchu and other ancient ruins nearby. The camera I had the first time was having issues, and I was able to get only two or three pictures. This time around I was able to see a few places in Cusco I hadn't been able to see before.

Later that afternoon I went to the travel agency where a friend worked to look at some tour packages and options. While I was talking with the agent there, my friend received a phone call from her brother. Their mother had been feeling ill and was on her way to the hospital. It made no sense for me to continue with my travel plans in light of this urgent situation. We went directly to the hospital. The family had invited me over for dinner the night before, so I knew everyone there. I spent several hours there just comforting my friend and spending time with her.

I'd gotten a few copies of some Bibles in Spanish before leaving on the trip, and I gave one to my friend's mother. She was very thankful. They were very devout in their Catholic faith but didn't read the Bible much. I didn't read anything to her; I just listened as she talked. I prayed with her before I left, a powerful moment.

We spent the rest of my five-day visit in Cusco. I had a lot of fun hanging around with locals, but I was not able to visit Machu Picchu again. I had come for sightseeing but had been used to meet the needs of people who needed it very much at the time. I was a bit disappointed about missing another opportunity to get pictures of Machu Picchu, but for the first time in my life I had put the good of others ahead of my own plans.

If we pay attention, God gives us a glimpse of what he has in store for us down the road. I wasn't paying attention then, although it is so evident looking back that this was the beginning of my call to the Andes.

CHAPTER 9

Dangers, Toils, and Snares

The makeshift desk in my room was always cluttered. I kept my laptop on my desk along with paper to write down phone numbers. Being in Caracas around the time that cell phones were gaining popularity, I still used a landline more than the cell phone I'd just bought. I did spend a lot of time on the phone setting up meetings and appointments.

One day I received a call with a special invitation. Enoch's church in Santa Barbara del Zulia had invited us as part of the university team to come and share with them. Our university work for the time being was limited to Caracas, but I jumped at every opportunity I got to share the work in other parts of the country and to talk about expanding the work in other universities around the country. A few tech schools in Santa Barbara wanted to start an English ministry. I was granted access to a car, so we headed out.

The drive would be eleven hours, clear across the country. We did most of the driving during daylight, but the last hour or two were in complete darkness. This would be a very brief trip, but we hoped to visit a few schools and talk to students.

We visited and shared with them for a few days before heading back to Caracas. A straight line would take us into the mountains, where we had never been, but we knew it would take time away from our trip. We didn't believe there was much to see up there anyway, so we decided to drive up the west coast of Lake Maracaibo and then to Caracas, the way we had come.

Enoch's cousin Yunior needed a ride to Lagunillas, about two hours up the lake coast and only a half hour out of our way, to attend a birthday party. This was another good reason to take the long way, around the mountains. I had never met anyone in this country named Yunior before. It is pronounced just like Junior. He was a nice kid, but until then I hadn't shared much with him.

The party started at four in the afternoon, so we waited until later to leave. We finally dropped Yunior off near the house. It was funny that having driven almost three hours with him, he just said just thanks and hopped out of the car and ran into the house as if we had given him a simple lift across town.

As we pulled out, I contemplated stopping in Cabimas for the night. It was still light, though, so we continued. I had to be back the next afternoon for an English class. Lagunillas is no more than forty-five minutes from Cabimas, and it would have been very easy finding a house to stay at there. Cabimas is on the highway that goes to Caracas, and a good night's sleep before getting on the highway would have helped. We continued toward Caracas and a few hours later were in Barquisimeto.

It was late and extremely dark. We were hungry, but the only thing open was a street vendor selling hot dogs. We sat in the car and ate, taking our time to rest a little before continuing. By then it was close to two in the morning, and we were still five hours from Caracas.

After resting for a while we left. A tollbooth marked the exit to the state of Lara, and we kept driving. Then I saw someone waving a white towel. As many there use that tactic to get people to stop their cars to later rob them, I didn't know what to make of this. Was he trying to rob us? In a matter of seconds I was able to see this was not a robbery. With little time to react, I saw what was really happening here. All I saw were axles and tires of a flipped truck in front of me, and I had no time to react to keep from crashing into them. Tiny pieces of shattered windshield glass struck me in the head as if shot out of a gun. I can't remember much else.

Several minutes later I gained awareness, marveling at the fact that we were still breathing. I remained conscious long enough to see that Enoch was all right and to see onlookers peering in. Even at that early hour and virtually in the middle of nowhere the road was filled with horrified bystanders. Each was recounting the events to the paramedics who were now there.

I don't remember the ambulance trip or the hours the doctors attended me. I remember only the missionary who appeared by my side after having driven several hours to be with me. My supervisor, Richard, arrived the next morning, and I was released from the hospital.

His reaction to seeing me was very calm. Maybe it was the anesthesia, but I didn't realize how much work the doctor had done. I was numb around my wound, so I felt very little pain. Miraculously I was in better physical shape than expected, but I was extremely discouraged. I still have scars from the more than two hundred stitches needed to sew me up that night.

I remember saying "Just let me go home." Knowing that this two-year apprenticeship was meant more for learning and adapting than for tangible results, Richard said that giving up would be to doubt what God could do through this unfortunate experience. Once again he was right.

I was very transparent about my feelings with Richard. It was no secret that I was embarrassed about my track record behind the wheel in Venezuela. The times I drove cars in Venezuela were few, and I had a near-perfect driving record back home, so it was very frustrating for me to have had so many accidents in Venezuela; from sliding on a wet spot in the road into a guardrail to being squeezed by a merging bus in rush hour to passing a slower car on the highway and getting hit by a car passing both of us, the freak incidents never seemed to stop.

The insecurity in Venezuela mixed with these curious occurrences was the substance of a process that humbled me like no other. Another lesson I learned through this was that God's presence can't fill someone who is filled with himself or herself. I was God's messenger, completely humbled to be filled with His presence. So many times I'd read passages in the Bible that spoke of humbleness, but you never really understand why it's so necessary until you live experiences that change you and allow you to grow.

Jesus came to earth to suffer and die, to show us the way to heaven, and to show us what pure love looks like. My sufferings in Venezuela led me to know a love I had never known before. All I suffered helped me identify with these people and to love them very deeply. It would be impossible for us to ever comprehend God's vast love for humanity, but I caught a foretaste of it through several near-death experiences in Venezuela.

Back in Caracas I was inundated by a flood of visits and phone calls from people who loved me and were concerned. Friends told me that their neighbors sent their wishes too. These neighbors had never met me and probably never would meet me, and yet they sent their best wishes, an overwhelming display of love. Wondering how such a poor decision like driving through the night on terrible highways could lead to such an outpouring of love helped me learn another lesson: we do nothing to deserve God's love; he just loves us unconditionally. Sometimes when we least deserve it, he shows it the most.

Our poor decisions lead us into trouble but never beyond God's love. On one occasion we were picking up a new missionary from the airport. She made the horrible mistake of stopping at an ATM for cash. We pulled into the mission office an hour or so later only to be robbed at gunpoint. Sensing that you really can trust no one in such a dangerous city, we had the suspicion that those who'd pointed the guns at us were off-duty police officers.

There's no justice in this world; there's only grace. One would think that having such a string of bad luck would turn some folks away from wanting to serve God, but these experiences were only further proof of his love and grace.

La Puerta

Having three English groups operating at the same time and planning social activities for each was starting to weigh heavily on me. I was delighted when Richard told me that some new missionaries were coming to help. Roland and Kathleen arrived four months apart about a year after me.

In addition to feeling a bit overwhelmed by the work, I was still recovering emotionally and physically from the accident. Having Roland and Kathleen to help was going to be a huge blessing. They were both new in the country when my accident took place, so I hated to welcome them on such a traumatic note.

Roland was a recent college graduate. He was much younger than Kathleen and me, who were about the same age. Each one had something unique to offer the team. We had little in common but were working toward a common goal. Weekly team meetings helped us to be on the same page tactically and to lift each other up in prayer.

Opportunities opened up for Roland to work at two new universities. God was blessing the work at the teachers' college, and Kathleen's help there with me was much needed and appreciated. She met the group there right away and got to know them very well. The group had several girls, and they were able to share more-intimate things with Kathleen, taking the pressure off me.

At one of our first planning meetings we got some exciting news. Our newly formed university team was headed to Mérida, the largest city in the Venezuelan Andes, about ten hours from Caracas, for a long weekend of meetings to share strategies and make plans with a large church-based ministry there.

Our limited time and our many meetings didn't allow me to experience much of Mérida. We stayed next door to where the meetings were, so we didn't venture out much. This didn't seem to affect Roland. He was extremely outgoing and made friends quickly. The contacts we met were valuable, and we were invited back. The weekend went by very fast, and without even time to unwind Richard told us that we would be leaving first thing in the morning for Caracas.

I remembered that members of the volunteer team from Mint Hill Baptist told me that Guillermo had been sent to La Puerta, a small Andean town half an hour from Valera, another major Andean city on the other side of the mountain from Mérida.

The group from Mint Hill Baptist had gone with him to visit when he was going there just on weekends and said it was a beautiful place. It was still around three hours from Mérida, but I couldn't be this close to my friend without visiting him. It was only slightly out of the way on my way to Caracas. Richard told me that it was okay to visit Guillermo if I could pay for the trip back to Caracas.

Taxis leave every two hours from the bus terminal in Mérida to head to the other side of the mountain to Valera. Leaving Mérida the next morning, the taxi headed upward toward the northern peaks. I saw the true meaning of the word *paramo*, and how it got its name.

In Venezuela, paramo, or "desolate land" is the term used to describe the high-elevation Andean areas, the mountain peaks above the tree line. I saw a dictionary definition of that word the first day. It is quite the opposite of Caracas and a contrast with the crowded shopping malls and baseball stadiums in New York. Another lesson I eventually learned was that God's love is as intense for one single person living in a scarcely populated place as it is for an entire city.

The full taxi moved fast as it maneuvered tight corners. The peaks we saw were upward of fifteen thousand feet with no trees or wildlife; a desolate but beautiful place. We stopped halfway at the Pico El Aguila, Eagle Peak. The café there sold the best hot chocolate. It wasn't a luxury, though; I needed it to warm up! A small statue of an eagle there helped me remember the name of the place. Across the road from the statue was a very small shrine. People were walking up to it, making the sign of the cross. They looked to whatever other statue was in there for guidance. This place belonged to God the Creator, but he did not yet belong to these people. We continued the trip a few minutes later. It would literally be all downhill from there, as we were now at the highest point of the trip.

As life slowly returned to the landscape I saw *frailejon*, plants unique to the high, northern Andean paramo. They grow where very few other plants can survive, and those on the paramo are protected by the Venezuelan government. They look like small bushes with long, thick leaves shooting out from the center. Their dark green color is effervescent, in contrast to the colorless landscape at this altitude. They were like celebrities here; tourists would stop along the roadside to get their picture taken with them. It was curious to think about where they came from or how they got there. The only conclusion one comes to is that they are God's gift to this place, a subtle reminder that life can exist in a place as remote and as barren as this.

This particular plant has baffled scientists for many years. Though it looks and functions much like a plant, some characteristics of the frailejon are still not understood. The plant has been named accurately all the way down to its genus, one step above the species level per the scientific nomenclature process, but it is given very generic species names in Venezuela, after the region it is found in.

Biologists believe that this particular genus evolved from another genus of plant that happened to migrate up the slope of the mountain. This hypothesis may be valid; when it comes to naming and understanding life, science is helpful, but we should always look to God the Creator to understand why on earth they even happen to be in this place. The question of how they exist so far up the mountain and how they sustain themselves baffles me, but why I was there, so far up the mountain, would soon be clear. The God who created it, and me, was calling me here.

The only explanation about the frailejon that makes sense is that God's hand sustains them. He put them here, and everything on this planet has a purpose, although many times we scratch our heads trying to understand what that purpose might be.

The frailejon were all over the Merida side of the mountain too. I must have been sleeping and missed them, as I had not yet gotten used to the thin air at the altitude. As we dropped in altitude, pine trees came into view. Houses just off the roadside started popping up, and we saw people at small kiosks selling coffee and souvenirs.

I didn't remember the names of any of the small towns we passed until we got to Timotes. It was a large farming town about an hour from Pico El Aguila. Entering Timotes, I asked the driver the best way to get to La Puerta. Good thing I asked, because he said small buses left right from here. Another passenger contradicted the driver and insisted I wait a bit longer to get out of Timotes and wait at a fork in the road they called the "Y" for a bus. It was easier to get to La Puerta from there, he said. The driver took that passenger's advice, typical of Venezuelan culture.

I got off at the Y and waited an hour and a half for any sort of transportation to pass. A bus heading to Timotes eventually came by and I hopped on. I made it to the bus small terminal, and a few minutes later I was off to La Puerta. It was the strangest thing, almost as if God wanted me to get a second look at Timotes, which turned out to be my future home.

Two hours later I arrived in La Puerta. It was so good to see Guillermo and his family after so much time. His two children were growing and adapting to a town completely different from Cabimas. I visited for two days with Guillermo and his family, and he shared his discouragement with me. He had been working there for about six months and had not seen many results. They were visiting a few families on a regular basis, but the church was not growing.

He had met two young people on one visit and was spending a lot of time with them. It was strange to see just the three of them sitting in that huge sanctuary. It was so spacious, and Guillermo's desire was to see it full on Sundays. That was not the case right then, but he continued to invest in Simon and Maritza, a young couple. They had just started to date and were getting serious. He was from a Christian home in the nearby town of Mendoza, and she lived with her family not far from the church. They were popular with the young people in town, but other kids had not started to show up at church. Not then anyway. Even though there was no numeric growth in the church, the two remained loyal to their times of study with Guillermo.

La Puerta means "the door." I was told that this village had been named by Simon Bolivar, Venezuela's liberator. He had seen that it was the doorway to the Andes, the longest mountain range in the world. It seems he was a man of vision, much like Guillermo. La Puerta is where the Andes start and where a tremendous missionary vision was born.

Mountain Vacation

Our university team met every Friday in the basement office below my apartment to share our experiences at the universities and discuss strategy for each one. Richard, Kathleen, Roland, and I, a formal team, planned and prayed as a group. Kathleen and I had something very important to discuss with the team on one particular Friday.

Each of my English groups in Caracas was bonding, and one day we decided to plan a trip with all of them. Guillermo really needed some help, and it was a great way for Kathleen to further bond with the university students we were meeting with twice a week. An adventure outside the city would help our group share a new experience and to bond further. It would also be a way for God to use this group in a unique way.

We presented our idea to Richard and the team and were met with an unexpected positive response. This would be the first time we would present the idea of working outside the city limits of Caracas, so we weren't sure if we would get the go ahead from Richard. Our supervisor, instead, applauded our outward focus and stressed how activities in other parts of the country were important even though our immediate work was in Caracas. The green light from Richard allowed us to tell our students and start planning. We were going to take my students to visit Guillermo.

We ended up planning a trip for Semana Santa, Holy Week, the week leading up to Easter, which is recognized by all Venezuela and is a vacation week for students and workers. My students from the teachers' college got on board with the idea, and students from several other groups also expressed interest.

Many of these students had traveled extensively throughout Venezuela, but many had not been to the Andes. These were mostly students from our Bible study groups, but since they were not all yet believers, this was more of a retreat than a real missionary trip. Regardless of the label we put on it, it was significant for many reasons, and God did something there that changed many of us forever.

Kathleen was wise to suggest that we rent a small bus with a driver. The cross-country trip was a blur; we spent it sleeping or playing word games in English to pass the time. This was before the onslaught of cell phones, so most of the time we were actually talking to one another and not texting, which helped us bond.

We were relieved to arrive in La Puerta after a twelve-hour, overnight trip. It took a while to get our sleeping arrangements settled, and by the time we did it was lunchtime. We shared a meal in the sanctuary of the church, and the students got to converse with Guillermo and his family.

That night we had the first Protestant church service some of our students had ever attended. They seemed to enjoy it, and many even said they wanted to go again sometime. It was not a private service for us, but besides a handful of townspeople we were the only ones there.

The church was in the center of town, but Guillermo was working in Pueblo Nuevo, a part of town quite a distance from the church. He began mostly visiting families and tending to their needs. Some of the girls who came with us on the trip had experience with hair styling and wanted to have a clinic there that week.

One family opened their doors to them, and they had some prospective students waiting to have a class. It was a great sharing experience for the people, for my students, and for Guillermo's wife, Elizabeth. We all learned a lesson that week: we all can find something we have in common with someone else, and that can be an awesome experience. It can be used to touch lives too.

Since our group consisted of students from different Caracas schools, many hadn't met each other before the trip. My disciple Dagmar met a young man on that trip who would open his heart to Christ at a church service. That was only the beginning of the blessings for him. They started dating shortly after that and got married a few years later.

Guillermo and I spent most of the week tending to the needs of the students and didn't have much time to talk. We were getting to know each other very well, and although he never said anything, I knew what he was thinking. He wanted me to come to La Puerta on a long-term basis to help him. Even with an almost-empty church he was going to need help. There was an overwhelming sense that something very big was going to happen in La Puerta.

It was difficult for us to return to Caracas, having bonded so quickly with everyone in La Puerta, but we left sad and teary eyed faces behind one Saturday morning. We were also crying; it was an emotional good-bye. My relationship with my English groups was never the same after that. We had shared an experience that had changed us. We were not just friends anymore; we were a tight-knit family.

Our normal work resumed in Caracas. Our day-to-day schedule was the same, but we were in a period of transition. I tried to teach Kathleen what the missionaries had taught me. My years in Caracas weren't necessarily meant to prepare me for a life of missionary service but to expose me to the missionary life.

My time in Caracas showed me what qualities were needed to succeed and what missionaries faced in the physical as well as the spiritual realm on the mission field. I learned many things about the Christian life and also about the importance of the church in my short time in Caracas that have molded my ministry and have changed the way I see people. I was happy to see Kathleen growing in those same qualities.

There were only a few months left in my internship; time to head home was fast approaching. Kathleen would do a fine job continuing the work, but I didn't want to leave my new family. I spent the next few weeks preparing Kathleen to accept the baton I'd be passing her. It was also a very emotional few months as I began to say good-bye to all my friends in the different groups and universities around the city. The day inevitably came, though, that I boarded an airplane for New York.

CHAPTER 12

Home

Heading through Caracas and out of the city, I tried to absorb all the sights one last time, not knowing if I would ever be back. Justin offered to stop for a moment so I could take pictures, but I told him no. The first tunnel came into view, taking us under Caricuao and a sea of shanty houses in that massive barrio.

The sunny Caribbean shone from a distance as we saw it through the end of the tunnel. Many ships were on the water, which looked calm from where we were. Five more tunnels eventually navigated us through the coastal mountains and to the airport. The city had been my home for the past two years, and I knew I'd miss it.

True to Justin's character and servant heart, he dropped me off at the curb and helped me with my bags. He went to park the car before meeting the rest of the group. Quite a sendoff awaited me. It was a bittersweet sendoff. I was going to miss my friends greatly but was anxious to see everyone in New York. An overwhelming number of Venezuelan friends and American missionaries were there to see me off. It was sad to leave, but the love I felt at that moment took the pain away. I hadn't been to New York in over two years and could not wait to see my family and friends. The plane would soon take off, and I'd be on my way, leaving a big part of me behind.

Venezuela is a large petroleum-producing nation. Its economy is driven by oil exports, but its poverty is obvious when you visit. The country's well-to-do people are not so evident, but they're there. Boarding the plane, I headed for coach, passing the first-class passengers, a majority of whom were Venezuelans. A feeling of inadequacy overcame me, and uncomfortable stares came from these more-fortunate passengers. These rich Venezuelans were going to the States for a long weekend, a trip any other person would have had to have saved months for. I couldn't help thinking that the fate we'll all meet at the end of this life is the same.

My family and a few friends were waiting for me at the Albany airport. My flight from JFK to Albany had been canceled, so I'd taken a shuttle from JFK to Albany. It was great to be home; they received me with hugs and balloons.

In New York I took time to regroup and see where to go from there. For a few days my life back home was exciting, and people were glad to see me. That quickly wore off, and it was time to find a job.

A specialized website for turf management led me to a job opportunity in New Jersey. I interviewed at a golf club and was hired as an assistant superintendent. As far as titles are concerned, this was the highest position I'd ever held on a golf course. The pay was great too. The emotion I had once felt, though, was no longer there. I went to work every day, worked long hours, and enjoyed it a lot. The original passion and drive I had felt in Charlotte, however, was gone.

A perk of the job was supervising some Peruvians on our crew. We had a blast talking in Spanish and sharing stories about different things. They thought it was so cool that I had been to their country. I thought my stories about Machu Picchu would be boring to them since they'd been there, but they seemed captivated by them.

My new friends would invite me out to eat Peruvian food with them, and they even helped me find an apartment nearby. I was spending a lot of time with my new work buddies. Opportunities to spend time with them were not lacking, and I found that opportunities to reach out to them would not be either. Every invitation they made I accepted, and it helped me get to know their needs.

Sharing with them about my missionary work in Venezuela allowed me to share with them about the Bible and to give them Bibles as gifts. This opened the door for questions and a chance to pray for them, something I began doing regularly. As most people from Latin cultures are very spontaneous, some impromptu Bible studies were started, and sometimes we would have almost twenty in attendance.

These were the people God had surrounded me with, but it was strange that I was in New Jersey teaching the Bible to a houseful of people from South America. I knew something as spontaneous as this would not have happened in American culture, so I treasured it.

At the time I was attending a rather large church in Patterson, New Jersey, which had a Hispanic ministry. I frequently had to work on weekends, so I attended Wednesday night services regularly. I shared with the pastor about the home where we had Bible studies, and the pastor offered to visit a family with me one day. It was amazing to hear him laying out the plan of salvation in broken Spanish. He was so enthusiastic about sharing with the woman who was there; his enthusiasm would have been lost in my translation. She accepted Jesus as her personal Savior, and it was a privilege to witness that moment.

A few from our group came to church with us at times. I'd leave the regular congregation to sit with them during the Spanish service. Regardless of the country or the culture, the mission of the church should never waver. The pastor and I shared the same sentiment that it was good to reach out to these families, but they needed to be plugged into a church. That was our plan, although very few actually continued to attend.

My friends in New York were far away, and we had little opportunity to keep in touch. Still as patriotic as ever, I had new friends but never forgot my roots. Tuesday morning, September 11th, 2001, reminded me again how great our country is.

Our golf course crew started work that morning very early as usual in perfect weather. Though summer was winding down, it was in full swing that glorious morning. I went out to cut cups for the holes and to check the condition of the greens. The dew burned off quickly, and the fine morning mist gave way to blue sky.

We normally took a break around 9:15 for coffee and a snack. The building we worked out of was behind the twelfth tee, far enough from the course to have privacy from golfers. We pulled up, and I saw my boss with a foursome of ladies in golf carts watching the news. The club was very exclusive and members rarely stopped; something was up. We sensed it was something bad that had happened, but we had a few more things to do to get ready for the day. We got back a few minutes later, and the crowd gathered around the television had grown.

Reports started coming in of two planes that had crashed into the World Trade Center. We were all stunned. No one talked. It was one of those moments in life when you never forget where you were. The television reporters did the best they could but had no new information. They were as shocked and as caught off-guard as the rest of us.

When Tower One fell, a woman in the maintenance shop let out a cry that moved everyone. It was hard to watch, but we had to. Everyone was confused; we had no idea what was happening. Reports started coming in about other planes involved and other sites targeted.

We stood there stunned, not knowing what to do. There was no news coming in for a few minutes, which translated into bad news. We did our best to keep our composure, but none of us really did. Our silence was as strong as the silence coming from the television.

It all moved very fast, and the news got worse by the second. My boss finally told us to call it a day and to go home to our families. I went home to Upstate New York to stay with my parents. The image of state troopers racing down the thruway toward New York City will stay with me forever.

I was home watching the news coverage and absorbing the events of the day when my mother came home from work. It wasn't my routine to check the answering machine, but she always did as she walked through the door. The answering machine had dozens of messages from friends in Venezuela who were worried about me.

Checking my e-mails, I also saw messages from other Venezuelan friends who were checking on me. I have friends and family here who hold me dear, but this love and concern went beyond what I experienced after the accident. It was special, to say the least.

I went to work the next day, and when I left that afternoon I drove to Hoboken, New Jersey. Smoke still poured from Lower Manhattan. I stood there with Gustavo, a coworker, praying for the firemen and the victims and for our country.

A few days later I stopped at a pharmacy to buy drinking water and other miscellaneous items to fill the back of my pickup truck. I drove through the Lincoln Tunnel to the Jacob Javitz Center in Manhattan. This was the main point of relief in New York City, where all sorts of donated items to help the survivors were being accepted. For only the second time in my life had I put others completely ahead of my own plans. Every single being who had breath in our country was united. Differences did not matter; we were one, and we were all God's creatures.

At times like that one can't help but contemplate a bigger picture. No one knew why this had happened, but my mind moved from my past life to eternal things. The career on the golf course I had once lived for no longer mattered to me. I was put on this earth to serve the living God and to follow his purpose for my life. Less than a year later, with a burden tugging relentlessly on my heartstrings, I resigned from my job and returned to Venezuela.

CHAPTER 13

Building Young
Missionaries

The fact that I couldn't be part of the church that had been constructed in Carorita, about twenty minutes straight up the hill from La Puerta, was always something that filled me with regret. Elizabeth, Guillermo's wife, passed around the pictures of the construction of the new church. It was amazing to see, but it always made me sad because during the time of the construction I'd been in the States, yet to be a part of this work in the mountains. These are experiences I had to live secondhand, but I have seen with my own eyes the results in this place.

I found a job as an English teacher at a grade school in Cabimas, involved in the Andean work only on weekends. I'd been on a few dates with a girl who lived in Cabimas, and we were interested in learning what might have been in store for us as a couple.

Guillermo offered me a salary for my work, but I decided to stay in Cabimas for the time being. A weekend with Guillermo can be as filled with excitement as a full workweek anywhere else anyway, so I was happy continuing like this for a while.

When he was first sent to La Puerta, Guillermo was able to travel there only on weekends as he had to tend to the congregation in Cabimas. The majority of the time the church had a padlock on it. A young American missionary and his bride from Maracaibo had gone to La Puerta a few months before and had found a padlock on the church there. It moved them greatly, and they were determined to find out more.

They had arrived there about a month before Guillermo was sent there permanently, not a coincidence by any stretch. They happened to meet Guillermo in Maracaibo through a mutual friend, and he shared about the struggles in the mountains, not just limited to La Puerta but also in all the Andes. The wept when Guillermo shared his vision for this region with them. A partnership was formed a few months later, and from that day forward the work in the mountains was never the same. I was happy to hear the news because Guillermo had been so discouraged when he'd first arrived in La Puerta.

The partnership consisted of several churches from different states in the United States. They came down two or three times a year with medical and construction teams and provided funding to send missionaries to different towns as well. I had been very happy to hear all this while I was in New Jersey. What I did not know was that Guillermo was looking for me, wanting me to be a part of it.

The work in the Venezuelan Andes had been lacking over the previous years. In this area of over two hundred square miles were only three Baptist churches. The leadership from the local church in La Puerta along with pastors from several churches in the United States prayed over goals that were possible to reach. With the number of people now involved, the ten-year goal they came up with was to start one hundred new churches in this area that spanned two states.

Most of the teens and young adults we had worked with two years earlier, when we had made that trip from Caracas, were now part of the church, so I'd be working with some familiar faces, which helped. The town was small, but there was enough to do. My new friends accompanied me wherever I went. The time not spent in La Puerta was spent in Carorita, a small farming community and the site of this amazing new church plant.

A family in Carorita stopped by the church to visit Guillermo. I don't know the details of the conversation, but the upshot was that the family desired to learn about God but found it difficult to make it down to church every Sunday. Guillermo's basic response was, "Where do you live? I will visit you there and share the Bible with you." A home church formed a few days later.

The group in Carorita was the apple of Guillermo's eye. It's hard to describe the special love he has for them, the image of the love God has for people. It started as something very special, and it still is. Guillermo grew this church from the ground up. He took part in building the church building, but he was also building young missionaries while he was at it.

You won't find paved roads in Carorita; everything is so spread out. There is no such thing as a "routine" visit to this place. A great lesson I learned through my experience of watching the Carorita church grow was who God used to grow it. The congregation of the church in La Puerta consisted of relatively new believers, but that didn't stop Guillermo. He brought young people from the church with him on every visit.

By this time, the young couple from La Puerta that Guillermo had invested so much time in had gotten married. They became the youth pastors in the La Puerta church. Simon, who loved to sing, was a vital part in getting many young people from La Puerta involved in the ministries of the church. Although Guillermo pastored the Carorita church, Simon's work with the youth was pivotal, and he eventually became Guillermo's assistant pastor.

The young people were involved in visitation and also in the construction of the church building there. They were building the church in every sense: they were feeding new believers with the truths they needed to grow, and they were involved in the physical building of the church sanctuary. The pictures shared with me show the joy on their faces as they dug the foundation and poured concrete. It was extremely hard work, but they seemed to enjoy every minute of it from the pictures I saw and the stories I heard. The beautiful church building has a unique design. I'm sad I missed out on its construction. It also blesses me to think that so much hard work went into this because the people in Carorita are loved greatly.

These young people got their hands dirty right away. The minute you begin a relationship with God, he wants to use you; there's no sitting on the sidelines. Many people disqualify themselves because they don't think they know enough, but these kids were so excited about being used that they got to work right away. None of us ever know enough, but I've seen God do too much through his people to use that as an excuse.

Guillermo and I visited six homes on average a day, and we walked to what seemed like the edge of the planet. These people were thrilled that people would make such an effort to visit them. They offered you everything they had. I learned my next lesson the hard way; never reject the hospitality of someone you are visiting.

As the sun was setting one day, Guillermo asked me to visit a new family in Carorita with him. When we visited a new family, it was just to show them we cared about them; we didn't go with an agenda; we went to listen to them and to get to know them. This family was precious. They were farmers, like most in Carorita, tending to land owned by someone else. The lady of the house was moved by our visit, and it was against their nature to not offer guests anything. She sent her son to get some fresh milk from her cow for us. My eyes widened; I knew I was in trouble. Guillermo, in a brief moment we were left alone, thought I should make an exception to the above rule for the sake of my health. But I was afraid that rejecting this offering might have shut the door for good on future opportunities to visit with this family.

I drank the milk and felt fine immediately afterward. I thought I'd dodged a bullet, but when I got home I started to feel the effects. The bacteria content of the milk was high, and they were foreign to my body. I spent the next week on Guillermo's couch, getting up only a handful of times. But, and a big but, it happened to be the week of the World Series, which I watched. To add insult to my injury, it was the 2004 World Series the Red Sox won in five games, the first World Series they'd won in almost ninety years.

Some things, like watching the Sox finally win the World Series, mark events in life. The lesson I learned was enough. I would never forget it, and it would mold my ministry. The price is a small one if it shows them love and opens the door for God to reside in their hearts.

Role Models

S tretched out on the couch, as if he were in his own house, Pastor Guillermo sat comfortably as he conversed with Maria. This was a quite normal occurrence when Guillermo visited homes. Maria brought us water and began talking about her stressful week. Guillermo listened intently. After a few minutes he assured her that God was concerned about her situation, and he shared some Bible verses with her.

The conversation was not a distant, overly religious one. The fact that he was sprawled out on the couch made it easier for Maria to open up to him. He had become someone very close to the family just by showing concern and listening to their needs, and in doing so he'd become one of them.

The fact that we believed gave us the responsibility to get to know people. Guillermo was from the city culture of Maracaibo, but you'd never know it when he dealt with people in the mountains. He found common ground with them immediately and connected with them. I know people who think that Christianity is too sanctimonious for them, but it couldn't be further from the truth.

One could certainly make the point that if God wants someone in a certain part of the world, he or she would simply be born there. It would have made sense for me to have been born and raised in the Andes if that was where God wanted me anyway. But if God had done it that way, I would have missed out on so many experiences that made me the person I am today. Our personalities are formed by our culture, our families, and our friends; our characters are formed by God.

I've been enriched by friendships that have given me a very well rounded taste in music, fanaticism for certain sports teams, and a sense of humor. On home visits in my ministry in Venezuela I've broached subjects ranging from American League pitchers' earned run averages to the influence of the Beatles on modern music. This helped me connect with them and lead to opportunities to share the truth of God's Word with them.

At Maria's house, Guillermo and I were a bit farther from La Puerta than some other communities we'd been visiting, but Guillermo had been invited by Maria to share with her family that day. Guillermo was never too busy to share with new people and expand the work farther up the mountain. The visit Guillermo and I made that day was the beginning of an exciting new church. After Maria had invited Guillermo to visit, he started doing so, building a close relationship with her family.

El Horno, "the oven," is a small farming community. The sun in the morning and early afternoon beats down on these homes pasted to the mountainside, and the heat is comparable with some coastal places in the country. It was a town with many physical and spiritual needs. It had been indifferent to the things of God for a long time, but we persisted with our visits.

The Apostle Paul will always be the example for missionaries. Walking the streets of Cabimas with Guillermo and reaching out to its people on my very first trip to Venezuela made what Paul did so many years ago very real to me. As I read about his ministry today, I find myself in awe, knowing how hard it is to connect with people from different backgrounds. His standard will stand forever. The accounts of Paul's life came alive when I observed Guillermo operate.

Paul, a man passionate and focused on growing God's kingdom, had a questionable past and had done some vile things to God's own people before his heart was changed. With his great example of missionary service we can learn many things. Paul said, "I am made all things to all men." He broadened his horizons to be able to connect with different types of people and share his faith with them.

It is amazing how different Venezuelans are from one city to the next. I used Paul and even Guillermo as my models; having a narrow world view would have been a disaster in Venezuela. Paul's example of how to adapt has been an inspiration to me, and I saw that lived out in Guillermo's life as well.

We need to heed the words of Matthew 7:13–14 that tell us to follow the straight and narrow path. God knows we can be easily tempted and go astray. Guillermo is a man completely devoted to God. He also has several interests, ranging from sports and food to travel, that he'd frequently bring up in conversation. He's an example of how being well rounded doesn't lead you further from God; rather, it helps you connect with people. He's not made the mistake of ignoring everyone and everything that may not be on the narrow path. There are people we meet every day in these mountains who are on a path leading to destruction, but we can't let them continue on it just because it might affect our righteous walk. After all, in his letter to the Corinthians, Paul exhorts them to preach Christ to all who are called, Jews and Greeks alike.

We always say we want to live for God, but what we do many times is strive to live a better Christian life for ourselves, thus eliminating the people who really need God from the equation. A prayer walk isn't done for our personal benefit; it is meant to explore and to put others' needs in God's hands. Our hikes in these mountains were a lot like that. They were not meant just to get ourselves in shape but to meet new people and begin praying for them.

Talking baseball with folks who live thousands of feet above sea level was not something I'd ever expected to do, but the people were as passionate and knowledgeable about the game as any rabid Yankees fan from the Bronx. I learned that my background and interests were as useful here as they were back home. Those who helped make me who I am today are just as much a part of my ministry here in the mountains as I am.

Growing up playing baseball and having attended many Major League games gave me the practical experiences to connect very quickly with these people. They asked me all the time what it was like to sit in the bleachers at Yankee Stadium. These conversations about baseball helped me build close friendships and helped open doors to invite many young people to church. I have learned to just be myself and let God do his work through me. The spiritual part of ministry comes from God anyway, not from us.

Our now dear brother Antonio was a man vehemently opposed to our work when we first started. The church in La Puerta continued their visits to his home to share with his wife and children, but Antonio wanted nothing to do with it. His indifference and opposition continued for several months until his daughter, who was married and lived in Maracaibo, came for a visit. Her husband, a Christian, got his father-in-law to attend church with them while they visited, and his heart was touched that day.

Antonio and Maria are not only regularly attending the El Horno church, they have also donated a house to the church. After some minor construction work the building got a new floor, a kitchen, and an expanded area for church services.

I believe that Antonio's heart change was a result of the many times Guillermo visited the family without ever pressuring him. He talked to them about life, and he let them get burdens off their chests. I wasn't part of the preliminary visits, but if they were anything like other visits Guillermo made, he may not have gone overboard with thoughts about God, but he always prayed for them at the end. I believe that because Antonio started feeling comfortable with Christians he finally accepted his daughter's and son-in-law's invitation to go to church.

I shared quite a bit with Antonio and Maria and learned that their son-in-law was a catcher in the Tampa Bay Rays minor league system. He was from Maracaibo, but I hadn't expected to ever have a baseball connection made between this town, which 99 percent of Venezuelans did not know existed, and Major League baseball. This led to several baseball conversations, showing me that things are not always one-dimensional. We shouldn't be that way as believers either. Working in this small village has taught me that we can always find common ground with others.

Johan Santana is a local legend in the state of Merida and a hero to many here. He was the phenom pitcher who propelled the Minnesota Twins to many winning seasons and is currently winding down his career with the Mets. The unexpected baseball conversation continued as they told me he was from a very small Andean town not far from them. It was fascinating for me to hear stories about this talented pitcher from Tovar, Merida. Building a strong relationship with them eventually allowed me to share with them about my hero from the equally small town of Bethlehem.

I've learned from Paul that the Gospel is for all who accept it. There is no reason I would spend the money I do, travel so much, and suffer things just to tell people that the Gospel is not for them but for only a select few. I have given the best years of my life to share a message quite the opposite: the Gospel is for everyone who accepts it.

CHAPTER 15

My Venezuelan Family

"If you go to the Andes, you're going alone." This was my girlfriend's reaction when I shared with her about the exciting opportunity to join Guillermo in this missionary effort in La Puerta. Besides Guillermo, pastors from the United States were insisting more and more that I go full-time in the work; they offered me a modest salary and housing. My girlfriend was probably hoping my interest would fade, but my passion for the Andean work grew.

We had been dating for a short time but had already started talking about getting married in the following year. We'd met on my first trip to Venezuela, and I'd seen the testimony of her family and their willingness to be used by God in different missions.

At first I was taken aback by her response. It was very hurtful to learn that she did not consider this opportunity as open for discussion. It wasn't her answer as much as it was the quickness of the response that hurt, a confirmation that she was not the one God intended for me. I had hoped that her passion for ministry in Cabimas would transfer to the mountains once she met the people. The large scope of what was happening in the mountains, however, was not important to her.

With overwhelming peace in my heart I had left my job in New Jersey and come here. I'd found a job as an English teacher and had plans to stay in Cabimas, working and helping my girlfriend's mother in a new church in town. Weekend involvement in the work in the mountains was fine for a while, but there was something drawing me back to full-time ministry. I was hoping my girlfriend would at least visit La Puerta with me, but that never happened.

I moved to La Puerta and began working with Guillermo and living in housing the church had built for missionaries in Pueblo Nuevo, where I'd been just two years before with my English students from Caracas.

My first roommate there was Ruben, a friend of mine for years. He worked with our group when we first were in Cabimas and had been working with Guillermo in La Puerta for a few months at that point. His talent with audio equipment was put to good use in La Puerta. He and I grew closer in La Puerta. He taught me a lot about audio-video work and how to set up microphones and sound systems, and he even made a pretty neat video about the work that had been started in the Andes. He was a tireless worker, something else that was rubbing off on us from spending so much time with Guillermo.

One year I got a cheap flight to spend some of the holiday season with my family. Ruben picked me up on New Year's Eve (New Year's Day, actually) at two in the morning to drive me to the airport for my flight to Miami when he could have easily stayed in Maracaibo with his family. New Year's celebrations are the same, maybe even a bit more intense, in Venezuela. His sacrifice spoke of his friendship and love for me.

Ruben, who got married and moved to Maracaibo, continues in the Andean missionary work during vacations from work and on long weekends. We're still as close as brothers; working with someone toward a common goal can bring people together.

Guillermo was also intensifying his leadership training with Simon and Maritza, the young couple who were youth pastors in La Puerta. Guillermo sent Simon to preach or lead Bible studies in different places when he was unable to. Simon's energy was infectious; he never stopped moving. People always remember his singing voice. He sang everywhere he went. He was a lot like Guillermo in that he liked to tell jokes. I think the only time he got serious was when he was behind a pulpit. I never knew if he was joking around with me otherwise, but when he preached God's Word he was solemn.

I'd grown very close to every young person in Pueblo Nuevo, a small group of homes stretched along a road running up the west end of La Puerta. The fact that all the kids there went to church made it possible for me to share a lot with them. In the afternoons I'd sit on porches at various homes and just watch kids play and cars go by. It made me feel at home, and even the adults liked hearing my stories about New York. It was an extremely long walk into town, so I stayed there a lot if I didn't need to be anywhere else. In a way, sitting on those porches and bonding with the folks was part of my job, although it didn't look like work.

God had given me a family of my own there, one with which I formed strong bonds. Their acceptance of me added enthusiasm to my work and made me feel at home. Being a part of this family has not made me forget my own family but has brought me closer to this place up on the mountain and has also motivated me to keep going.

Venezuelan missionaries had come from Guarico, the plains area of the country almost ten hours away, to work with us in La Puerta. The local missionary agency that formed from the partnership with the stateside churches gelled quickly as a family. The team was made up of missionaries and pastors from different backgrounds and places and started ministering in towns throughout the mountains. Every baptism, every wedding, every funeral was an experience that all shared. I will belong to this fraternity for all my remaining years.

Having proposed to my girlfriend just a few months earlier, I thought the Venezuelan family I would eventually have would be a literal one, complete with children and in-laws. I'm still waiting to raise a physical family and still find myself a bit sad for how things worked out between my girlfriend and me, but I see now that the missionaries I work with are a family God has intended me to have all along, and I couldn't be more thankful for this family I have been given and for the vision that unites us. Such bonds can never be broken.

CHAPTER 16

A Bountiful Harvest

Missionary work is primarily focused on evangelism and church planting. While this is important, meeting physical needs is also something important, which is why a good portion of missionary work has a humanitarian aspect as well.

Construction projects and medical teams were part of this effort to partner churches in the mountains. I was soon taking part in another humanitarian project with a very special person filled with God's love.

On one of the teams that came down to visit La Puerta was an agronomist with a vision to help farmers. Gorden was looking for an interpreter, but they could not find one familiar enough with farming terms. Much to their surprise, my background was exactly what they needed. This partnership began around the time I'd returned to Venezuela. God was working everything out.

This agronomist invited me to join him on a brief tour of two or three towns in the mountain's higher region. Pastors there were organizing soil seminars for the farmers in each town, and Gorden and I were to speak to hundreds of farmers and their families. The trip was a huge success, and many new contacts were made.

I was to work as Gorden's interpreter two times a year at most, but someone who could speak Spanish and also "farm" had to follow up with the farmers.

We planned visits and activities for Gorden when he would return for two weeks at a time. He'd fallen in love with Pueblo Llano, a town about four hours from La Puerta. He was very impressed with the farmers there and the amount of carrots and potatoes they produced. The pastor there was a servant who loved people.

We affectionately came to know Pueblo Llano, or "plains town," as Pueblo Lejos, or "far town," since it took time to get there from La Puerta. The weather there almost all year 'round is that of a late autumn day: gloomy, cloudy, and cold. Its pastor had fallen ill and was going home to battle cancer. Sadly, some of his physicians think that the tremendous amount of pesticides used in the area may have had a part in making him sick.

But his illness didn't stop him from getting people to go to the seminar. It was a shock to find that the attendance of our first soil seminar was four hundred people. This pastor had certainly done his work and had half the town there. It amazed me that nerves did not bother me at all that night as I translated Gorden's presentation.

We had arrived in Pueblo Llano at night, but the morning we left we saw the characteristic of Pueblo Llano the town was named after. It is nestled in a wide mountain valley and seems to have no end. Houses are spread throughout it like patchwork. As you make your way through the plain, countless motorcycles pass you. They are the easiest way to get around here since the narrow roads are filled with flatbed trucks filled with freshly harvested produce.

Among many curious things in Pueblo Llano are the washbasins for carrots. The look like handball courts you see in inner city parks but with a basketball-sized hole in the middle. High-pressure hoses spray the freshly picked carrots to wash off the dirt and chemicals. As the water pushes the carrots through the opening, men on the other side bag them for market. The town, which appears lifeless as you drive through it, produces more vegetables than any other town in the country even though most Venezuelans couldn't find it on a map.

These trips around the mountain helped us build an intimate relationship with the place. We were becoming familiar with its many small towns and villages, but it was still easy to get lost.

One day, Gorden and I were visiting some new towns, preparing for one of his soil seminars that evening. We visited several farms that day and traveled very far from Pueblo Llano. We had to head out to make it back on time, but Gorden wanted to visit one more farmer to get some added insight to this area. His wife saw a group of houses just over the horizon, seemingly just minutes away, but our driver told us, "That town is three hours away." It seemed so close in our eyes, but in reality it was not.

Our classmates and coworkers seemed so close sometimes; seeing them every day. In reality they couldn't be further from us. I always tried to bridge the gap by simply sharing my faith with people, which seems admirable, but I see now that throwing Bible verses at them without getting to know them created a valley that continues to grow We got to know those mountains and the roads around them well by simply exploring them and getting to know them.

Another town we visited was San Rafael de Mucuchíes, the highest-altitude organized town in Venezuela. Mostly potatoes were grown there, and its congregation was new and growing. We really got to know the farmers well in all these towns; some would stick around after the seminars and pick Gorden's brain. He loved this, but it was tiring for me as the translator. These times were valuable to the ministry but seemed to go on forever.

A town we also visited the first time Gorden was here and where we'd seen a good response was Timotes. Its church had a new pastor with whom we worked to plan another soil seminar. His was one of the three original churches in the area, and its membership was made up almost one hundred percent of farmers. It would make sense to have an agricultural outreach going on there.

Gorden shared the importance of biblical stewardship of the land when he shared with these farmers. They had begun implementing suggestions Gorden had left with them on a previous visit and had experienced a significant increase in yield.

Our relationship with Gorden grew, and the farmers asked about him constantly. We had stumbled upon something big, and people were responding to it. Our brother had a business to attend to back home, so unfortunately he was able to come down only once every few months.

A few months later Gorden made an unannounced visit. He wanted to share something that had been on his mind for a while, setting up a full-time agricultural outreach in the Andes. His home church was onboard with the idea and would back it financially.

Ruben and I went to Maracaibo to pick up Gorden and his wife, Shirley, and take them up the mountain. We met Guillermo, who happened to be in Timotes, to listen to Gordon's ideas. Gorden shared his vision to continue his soil seminars and also launch a ministry that would train a select group of farmers to be sent out as well to visit towns that we would never have had time to visit if he continued coming to Venezuela only once or twice a year. I was going to be the one training these farmers, a lot of responsibility.

Our new team was going to send soil samples to a university to be studied. The Venezuelan Andes span three states and close to two hundred square miles, and Gorden wanted to reach every town. We needed to find a location central to many of the places we were already working but close enough to La Puerta to make communication and meetings easier. Considering the geography and logistics, Timotes was the perfect place. With a new, enthusiastic pastor and a growing congregation of mostly farmers it made perfect sense. I would be moving to Timotes to begin this new, exciting work.

Gorden gave me an intensive training course in how to select and train team members. Having been his interpreter and having had my golf-course experience helped, but there was more to learn. A few months later I visited Gorden in Illinois to begin learning what I needed to, and I visited his church, which had supported our Andean work for so long.

It is always good to be in the United States. God had given me sufficient grace and peace to be overseas, but I liked being home. Even a trip to Dunkin' Donuts was a treat. Ordering food in English, watching golf on television, and mowing grass were things I'd missed so much. I spent three months with Gordon, living in a camper behind his house, until he was satisfied I could share his knowledge with the people in the mountains.

Our mentor-student relationship was a good example of discipleship. Gorden was pouring his years of farming knowledge into me with the faith that I would find the right men in Timotes to teach as well. We spent time in prayer, too, asking God to lead us to these men. When we finished, there was no graduation, but Gorden was a father, so he had words of wisdom for me before sending me off. "I want you to go and spend time with your family in New York before heading back to Venezuela. It would be good for you and for them."

My visit to New York was good. My family was used to having me around only for short periods, but the time spent with them was always a blessing. Family is where it all begins and ends for me regardless of where I travel. Gorden helped affirm that lesson for me, and I thank God every day for my family.

Autoridad

I headed back to Venezuela. When I arrived in the mountains, I spent one night in La Puerta before embarking on my new adventure. I'd been staying in the missionary house for a very long time but had no furniture of my own, nothing to move. I lived out of a backpack. Even in Timotes I had to stay on the first floor of Pastor Angel's two-story house. The first floor had been the church sanctuary until the congregation outgrew the building.

Pastor Angel was replacing a pastor who was leaving to lead a church in Caracas. Pastor Angel was the right man for the job; he was there right when God needed him to be. Angel and his family arrived in Timotes from Maracaibo when the partnership began with the churches in the United States. The timing and how it all worked out only confirmed Angel's call to that place.

Three of his four children were in college, so he and his wife, Maritza, faced many financial challenges. Blessings poured into his household, however, because he put complete trust in God. His children in college never had to call and beg for money because their father had instilled in them the same faith in God's provision.

Though Pastor Angel was not a dictator in his home, his family submitted to his leadership. The church family witnessed this as they saw firsthand how the pastor's family was sustained by God because they were united under Angel's leadership. Maritza spoke her mind and made household decisions, but she knew blessings flowed into the home through man's obedience to God. Maritza used that knowledge to guide the women of the church, helping them build better family relationships. Living so close to them for several years, I too learned that leadership is also following and helping others around us move forward.

Pastor Angel set aside a few days a week to visit people. While he recognized the importance of visitation, he didn't visit as much as Guillermo did. One thing Angel and his family did more than anyone else was open their home to others. It was rare to ever see that house empty. Teens and adults alike were there sharing with their pastor and asking him questions.

During the few short months I lived below them, my hot water heater rarely worked. They'd have me come up to shower and then have breakfast with them. At first I thought it was a bit of an invasion of privacy, but they insisted on it. Maritza served us black coffee with a lot of sugar. I'd grown accustomed to drinking coffee with cream in Caracas, but to this day I drink black coffee. (I've cut down on the sugar I put in it though).

Even with so many people in and out of that house, Angel always had sufficient quiet time with God. He'd never miss out on that because he knew how important it was. He put his time with God ahead of everything, but he also knew that the people had urgent needs. They were visiting because they needed someone, and he always made himself available. Maritza did the same for the women when Angel was traveling.

He and his family learned quickly that they were in a place of immense physical beauty. The beauty never wears off, but it becomes extremely difficult to live there once the first days are over as life's challenges set in. Families and individuals, even in a paradise like this one, still had struggles and problems and were in need of spiritual guidance. These suffering people were the reason they had come here, not just to admire the beauty of the mountains. When the realization sets in that they're here for the long haul, people become the priority over sights as breathtaking as they were.

Being a born leader, Pastor Angel first looked for the men who would be working alongside him. He took the time to get to know them, observe their talents and gifts, and gauge their desire to see the ministry flourish. After identifying some men, he started meeting with them regularly. The majority lived on the hillside , and the pastor went up every two weeks to meet with the group at the home of Marcelina and Armando, people with whom I shared coffee and conversation.

The trek to get to this home showed the dedication of these men. Those who lived down the hill had to first make it up the hill and then navigate a narrow footpath around a valley stream in the dark. Once they made it that far, they had to cross a man-made bridge with no borders to finally make it to the house. The water moved extremely fast under this bridge! It was a path I took often to visit these folks, one I got used to, but I was always impressed with it. A flat area near the bridge was where we started baptizing believers.

Pastor Angel would always have a theme he wanted to discuss with us and a brief Bible study to drive home his points. These times built these men up and prepared them for the job ahead. The fellowship time, having us all together on Thursday nights, was priceless.

These men were extremely well versed in the Scriptures. They had been members of this church since they'd been kids. Even with their extensive Bible knowledge they realized God had called them to follow a man to whom God had given a vision. They didn't assume their Bible knowledge and time in church qualified them to head these efforts.

Pastor Angel was the new guy, still in the process of adapting to the Andean culture, but that didn't matter to these men because of their spiritual maturity. They recognized that since Angel had been called there, the authority was his immediately, no questions asked.

This was the right time and place for Angel and his family for a few reasons. His family was extremely united and extremely devoted to the things of God . They have been an example in Timotes now for many years. But the main reason this was the preordained time and place for Pastor Angel was a question of culture. The culture in the mountains is very reserved, and the people are quiet. Children as well as adults are addressed in formal Spanish. The culture in Maracaibo, on the other hand, is an "in your face" culture in which people speak their minds no matter what. And they speak their minds about *everything*. To accomplish what needed to be done, things had to be addressed without kid gloves. Pastor Angel was filled with the love of God but went in swinging as he dealt with these men.

Just like Jesus has also said regarding his own ministry, the pastor held the stance that people in Timotes were either going to be for him or against him. He eliminated all fence sitters. Some who had been leaders in the church left, while others embraced him and committed to being more involved. Angel received the authority God had given him. His position of authority gave him a position of a bit more accountability, so technically he held a higher position than the rest. He didn't sit on a high place and look down on others; he got on their level, and his decision to do so paid great dividends. Ministry is about people, and Pastor Angel led his flock not always where they wanted to go but where they needed to go.

The best years of my life have been in Timotes, and not just because of what I have seen God do there through this once-small congregation but for the deep connection we now have. Pastor Angel was the glue that brought us all together.

Our Team

I can't say the church members in Timotes were people I knew very well when I moved there. The farmers were happy to have me at first; I represented free labor. Most days I spent working alongside them watering, weeding, harvesting, whatever they needed done.

During this process I was not only getting back into very good physical shape, but God was revealing the right people who would be a good fit for the team. Hildemaro was the first one I picked for our agricultural team. I would stop by his house sometimes late in the afternoon after he returned from the fields to share soil test results with him or make plans. This was the only time I had to share with him, and our meetings were always brief. I didn't want to impose on his time with his family, but as I sat down to talk with him, his wife would bring us coffee, and one of the kids would climb up on my lap. Their mother would always say, "Don't bother Mateo like that," but I didn't mind; it made me feel at home.

We would talk for several minutes, and Hildemaro would intentionally extend the conversation. When I tried to excuse myself, he'd ask, "Where are you going? Don't go home yet. Stay for a while." A few minutes later his wife would call us into the kitchen to eat. The women always wait to eat last in Andean culture, and that always made me a little uncomfortable. They had worked hard to prepare meals but had to wait the longest to enjoy them.

Mateo was one of the leaders who returned to the church to work with Pastor Angel. My friendship with Mateo has grown so much since the day we met way up on the mountain. He'd been away from church for a few years, but the pastor had him high on the list of men to visit upon arriving in Timotes. Mateo has been a man God has used tremendously in the vision he has given us in these mountains. Choosing him as the second member of this team was a no-brainer.

His wife, Rosa, is from Maracaibo and speaks a lot like Pastor Angel, who is also from there. People from Maracaibo speak distinctively from everyone else in town. This family loved to have me for dinner. I would see her from time to time in town at the market or at the bakery and she would just ask "Que dia, Matthews?" and giggle. It was her best attempt at pronouncing my name in English and a way of asking me what day I was coming to their house to eat.

Those visits allowed me to share a lot with them, and I came to see that Mateo, my *tocayo*, (a Spanish word for people who share the same name) have been united in this great purpose of seeing this paramo return to its Creator. His daughter has married one of the many young men from the church who have been called to be a missionary. They are pastoring a new church close to Timotes.

Working twelve hour days alongside the farmers allowed me to get to know them. When I first started helping them harvest, I thought it would allow me to get down to their level; in reality I was lifted to a higher level. These men worked hard for their families and for the owners of the land they kept.

I would go home dirty and completely worn out after working with them. It wasn't too bad, as I was young. The amazing thing was that not only did these men do this every single day of their lives, some of them were twice my age, and they didn't use tractors; they spent the entire day on their feet, carrying crates of lettuce or beets. It made my days stacking wood in the backyard with my father seem like play. These men would shake your hand with hands calloused by years of work. One of the hardest things to believe is that they still worked with oxen, and I know from firsthand experience it's strenuous work that requires skill, patience, and perseverance. It's an art that required years of dedication and learning, but they did it well. It was almost a way they worshiped God.

The farmers who were also leaders in the church worked as hard in their new responsibilities as they did on their farms. It is because of their hard work and dedication that the church has seen tremendous growth. Not only has the main congregation grown, but other communities around Timotes now have churches because of their efforts. God did all this, but he used men and women to achieve it.

We are fulfilled when we are working, and I am thankful for the work ethic my father instilled in me. One thing I learned by working alongside these farmers, though, was that when it comes to physical labor your muscles are important. When it comes to serving God in ministry, all you need to do is obey Him and those he has put above you. The rest isn't even work—it's all blessing.

The decision about whom to choose was not just a matter of their knowledge and ability but also their willingness to be part of the team. I was able to verify these qualities just working alongside them and talking with them in the fields. The orders I had been given were to pick three men. There was enough financial support to offer them a small stipend for travel and time away from their farms.

I picked Hildemaro and Mateo based on their years of experience in farming and in ministry. I picked Honorio because of his desire to be part of this work. He took time just about every day to ask questions and learn from working in the fields with us. The completed team started meeting three times a week for study.

About a week or so into the study we took a field trip to a farm in town where we took our first soil sample and talked at length with the workers about fertilizers and soil conditions. It served as a great icebreaker for both parties. People in the Andes are very shy and reserved. The farmers would talk to each other at the supply store or where they sold their produce but would rarely visit other farms.

The field trips became more and more frequent and we started visiting populations outside Timotes. The pattern was always the same; we'd offer to conduct soil studies and chat with them about their harvests and the problems they were facing. The specifics our team members were learning in our studies helped, and at times they would chime in on their own and ask farmers about their calcium or nitrogen levels. This helped their credibility; most farmers in the area just applied what the suppliers told them to. The team members found that such conversations were great ways to open doors of communication and further opportunities to share. We can always find something in common with someone. To meet their spiritual and physical needs we have to start with common interests.

Some challenges faced us as we began to function as a team. The university that analyzed our soil samples was two hours away. We had no way of knowing if someone would be there to accept the samples, and sometimes we lost complete days going to the university just to find out it or sometimes just the soil lab was closed for whatever reason. And while technology was very reliable in Venezuela, this wasn't the case in the mountains. We accessed the Internet by slow, dial-up service that came and went. It was the only way I had to get Gordon the results of the soil tests. The challenges didn't hinder us, however; we kept moving forward.

The agricultural ministry was in full swing, and most of my time was spent talking with farmers and working alongside them. It was an opportunity to observe how they prepared the ground, how they planted, and how they harvested. It was also an opportunity to observe how they dealt with challenges. I learned how the two-season year, the rainy season and the drought season, affected crops. Each season brought a different challenge. Rain is a good thing if you want to enjoy a healthy yield, but too much can be a hindrance. When it rains every day for weeks on end, the farmers can't work, and their crops sometimes get washed out. And during times of drought, people on the mountain go to great lengths to conserve water on the farms and their homes as well.

The farmers were a great inspiration to me. When they were unable to work in the fields, they spent their days maintaining their vehicles and other equipment. Regardless of the challenges the weather brought, they never stopped working. During times of spiritual drought, too, we have to keep moving forward even when God seems far away. During these times we need a strong family.

Timotes

I always have to fight back tears when I hear "Gloria Al Bravo Pueblo," the Venezuelan National Anthem, and one day I heard sixth graders sing it at their graduation ceremony. I'd been invited by their teacher as I'd spent most of the year sharing English lessons with the group.

The ceremony was long, but I silently applaud as each of "my" kids passed by to receive a diploma on stage. I was going to miss them, but it was a joyous occasion as they were going to be starting new chapters in their lives in junior high. Being one of their teachers had been a privilege, one that made me feel part of the community.

I was getting to know the people in Timotes well. After I'd lived there a few months, some women in the church asked me to help their children with English. Every Tuesday and Friday I walked to the school to give a two-hour English lesson.

There are some vast differences between public schools in Venezuela and the United States. Venezuelan school children wear uniforms, and they don't slouch in their chairs but sit up straight. They are hardly ever disrespectful and greet you when you walk in the room. *Buenos dias, profe* was the greeting I received my first day, and after that it came in English: "Good morning, teacher." To this day many greet me with *Hola, profe* when I'm in Timotes.

We had so much fun in that class singing songs and playing games as the kids were learning English, and they were always curious to learn more. They passed their tests with flying colors. We were together for a whole school year until they graduated.

Another great opportunity that opened up for me was to move up the hill, closer to our team members. Houses in Timotes are spread up and down the valley, and some church members lived on the east side of the valley. It was quite a walk from the pastor's house, but I did it every day. This invitation to live with them was an honor.

The American missionary who had founded the church many years earlier had been the last nonnative to live there. Between this special invitation and the fact that the thin mountain air no longer bothered me, I felt I was becoming one of them.

Up on the hill, families build houses for their children, close to them so when they marry they're able to stay and work the lands with them. One resident, Vicente, had a house he was willing to rent to me at a very reasonable price. Because I was living so close to him and his family, I got to know them very well and took part in everything his family did.

Vicente and his wife, Alejandra, have four sons. Evaristo, Joaquin, and Jhonattan were single and lived with them. Gregorio, who had been married for several years, lived just across the road. I spent every day with them between church and working with them on the farms.

As a routine every morning (the roosters would wake us up at five), I would go down and have coffee served by Miss Alejandra. She always made coffee and breakfast for her husband and sons. Their adopted daughter, who was married and living in Valera, visited every weekend, so I became her sixth child. Every morning she would say, "Don't forget to come back and eat breakfast."

The boys knew every inch of the paramo around Timotes. Over coffee we'd discuss different hikes they wanted to take me on. Jhonattan, the youngest, was the most adventurous by far. "Mateo, next week we are going up there," and he would point to a spot far up on the mountain. He was true to his word; he'd take me there and get me back without ever getting lost.

Well, we did get lost one time, but it was because he wanted to fish and lost track of where he was. The trail we'd left to get to the fishing stream was far behind us. In his haste to catch a lot of fish he barely got us back before dark. We did have a great dinner that night, though.

Timotes, an extremely narrow village, runs for about six miles up a mountain valley. While homes are scattered all over the hillside, the town is mostly in the valley, and that's where most of the businesses are. There were many places to explore, and we did just that.

Timotes is about ten miles from Eagle Peak, but because of a curvy road it takes about an hour by car. Cold mountain nights put frost on the crops some mornings. Farms made the landscape look like a patchwork quilt. Locals would head up the mountain en masse during July and August, wintertime, to see the snowfall on the peak. It was something very exciting for them, although come February when I was in New York we could do without more snow.

For those who came from Maracaibo and Caracas to work with us, the cool air was a great reprieve from the stuffy heat of the coastal areas. Climate was a factor our ministry used to its advantage, but we wanted people to come for the right reasons, not just to beat the heat.

Winter hats were accepted apparel, but as a rule locals never wore gloves. That was explained to me after several family members back home generously sent me gloves for some children in the paramo. The kids were nonetheless thrilled with the gloves and used them when they went to see the *nevadas*, the snowfalls on the peak.

I'm glad these gifts were put to good use. No gift should go unappreciated, and it was great to see the pure joy on the faces of these kids. When we give generously, there is always someone who benefits from it. It is the giver who is blessed by his or her kind act.

Friends and family sent me cold-weather clothes. It was just a matter of giving what was needed the most, although the giver's heart and intentions are more important than the gift. Sweaters and heavy insulated boots worked great for our hikes as it got unbearably cold on the peaks, especially with the wind.

The church in Timotes consisted mostly of members of two families related by marriage. They occupy many of the homes up on the hill where I lived. My house was always safe when I had to travel; they looked out for it. I had immediately become one of them.

The house had farmland literally on its front steps. One time I came home from a long trip and the boys said to me, "We just harvested some cilantro and put it in your living room. Hope you don't mind." They'd put several baskets of cilantro in the living room, but I didn't mind at all. It smelled wonderful. The nighttime temperature in Timotes was perfect for the cilantro anyway.

These people on the hill have shown me so much love. A different home would invite me to dinner every night. They were well aware that between my salary as an English teacher and the stateside support I was receiving I could buy my own food and prepare it. But they knew, and I eventually learned, that people get to know each other quicker when they are servants to each other.

I almost felt like I needed a doctor's note to excuse me from dinner if I couldn't make it. For reasons I didn't expect and certainly didn't understand, I was part of this extended family up on the hill, and there was no turning back. As much as I didn't expect or understand it, I deserved it even less. The people in Timotes were now my family, and they loved me unconditionally.

School in the Clouds

The aromas of smoke from the wood fire and of coffee welcomed me every morning in Miss Alejandra's kitchen. The cement floors were cold even with the fire burning a few feet away. She'd warm the coffee and fire up the gas stove to prepare arepas.

"Buenos dias, como amenecio usted?" The matriarch would ask me in her gentle and timid voice how I found myself any one morning. "Buenos días, hermana, bien, y usted?" I'd reply. It was very early, and Evaristo and I were drinking coffee before he was going to water the cabbage crop in front of my house.

A few minutes later Jhonattan bounded in as if it were midday, having come back from feeding his horses. "Buenos dias, Mateo!" he shouted as if to wake anyone still asleep. His youthful enthusiasm was needed that early and was something I'd grown to appreciate, but his mother scolded him for the noise.

Jhonattan, Evaristo, Joaquin, and I regularly planned our hikes over breakfast. Gregorio, though married, participated too, getting up early to take us in his truck to give us a head start. It was so much fun to be with them; we were bonding and growing closer with each hike, which we eventually combined with ministry. I'd always asked them what was on the other side of the west mountain. Their response was always a humorous "Lots of stuff," and it always left me curious.

One day we went there on a two-day hike that we turned into a prayer walk. On the other side was Piñango, a very small community. I was shocked when they told me that Piñango was there, since there were signs for it on Eagle Peak, and a road just past the peak led there. It was fascinating to think of how these mountains made things that were really so far away seem much closer. It was a dream for me to see Piñango; I'd been praying every day for an opportunity to visit it and eventually start a church there.

They had all been there and said that if we were able to make it there in one day that there were places for us to sleep. *Posadas*, or bed and breakfasts, are very popular and reasonable tourist destinations in the Andes, but it was hard for me to believe that there would be posadas in such a remote place. I'd forgotten that the road from the peak made the town more accessible, but walking there would be a full day even with Gregorio giving us a ride halfway up the mountain.

There were no sights to take in at the early hour we left. It was hazy, and the sky was dark. We began the hike before daybreak. When the sun peeked out of the clouds a few hours later, I couldn't believe my eyes. The view was incredible. We were too far up to see Timotes, but we could see peaks and valleys miles away. The sun rising over the hills and valleys was a wonderful welcome to that new day and the adventure it brought with it.

What I saw next amazed me: a school. Considering the number of homes spread over the mountaintop, there must have been enough children to fill the small building. The sight brought me back home for a brief moment as I saw mothers walking their little ones with lunch pails and book bags to school. All up and down the eastern hemisphere mothers and fathers were doing the same thing at that same time. A school

I had no idea existed just the day before was going through the same morning routine that was practiced in even the largest of cities, but I was sure that education in the one-room schoolhouse I saw was quite different. The kids still wore uniforms though, a part of the culture that impressed me so much. I immediately voiced interest in visiting this school in the clouds to share English lessons or stories about my life back home. The boys said that another visit could be arranged.

The boys also told me the name of this area of spread-out homes was Tafallez, a name I still think is fun to pronounce. The double "l" in Spanish is like our "j," so it is pronounced "Taf-a-jays." Even though this was a remote area, we could start praying for its people.

I was doing what any missionary should do, going to the ends of the earth to help mankind. It wasn't something that made me feel good, though, as I began to think of my past. It started to weigh heavily on my mind that I had not once visited my neighbors back home or even invited them to church.

This thought taught me another lesson: we all know the truth about ourselves. We try our best to maintain the appearance of holiness, but our error in trying to do this is that we fail to recognize that holiness comes from seeking greater intimacy with God. If we seek to simply have an appearance of holiness, it will be empty, and those around us will know.

The Bible reveals what we need to change. We tend to use the Bible instead to point fingers when God's desire is to gently bring to light the things we need to change. I went from feeling bad about past failures to being filled with joy for having been given the new opportunity to serve God during our hike.

The ride Gregorio had given us had been a good head start; it allowed us to make the trip in a day. It was literally all downhill once we reached the top. It was actually easier at times given the terrain to jog. That allowed the weight we were carrying to take us on pure momentum. It was not hard to keep control of our bodies, and we started to race each other.

These brothers loved each other, but like all brothers they didn't always show it. Jhonattan and Evaristo let me in on a trick they were going to play on Joaquin. The evil schemes were mostly always Jhonattan's ideas he'd coerce others into going along with. Evaristo and Jhonattan were carrying all the food, and they knew Joaquin became very irritable when he got hungry. The plan was to run ahead and hide from Joaquin. We were halfway through lunch when he finally caught up with us. He was not happy. "Why did you do that? I'm *hungry!*"

Joaquin's story is absolutely powerful. He was a young man with a speech impediment and obvious physical limitations still living to worship God. Moving to Timotes afforded me the opportunity to get to know him, share with him, and witness his miracle.

On many of our hikes Evaristo and Jhonattan really let their brother have it. They made fun of him a lot. It was all in good fun, but sometimes lines were crossed. Everyone loved him but still pointed out his shortcomings.

Joaquin shared with me on several occasions his desire to marry and have a family. "Good" Christians try to say the right things. I would say to him, "Keep praying for that" or "You know with God all things are possible." But I thought it a stretch of faith to imagine he would ever find a wife. Even his family expected to have him living with them forever. I was renting a house that actually belonged to him. I was approached many times about the possibility of buying it from them, since they thought Joaquin would never need it for his own family. But Joaquin never stopped praying, asking God for a wife.

It is because of Joaquin that I now know what true worship looks like. He was so spontaneous during church services. He would approach the musicians, and they would start playing a song without ever having rehearsed it, and Joaquin would sing his heart out to God. It left the congregation in tears many times, it was such a blessing. During the first two years

I knew him I was transformed from someone deathly afraid to sing even in a choir to standing with Joaquin and singing to the Lord. I love Joaquin as if he were my own son. I thank God for him, and I also thank Him for giving him a wife and a family.

On that hike we made it to Piñango a few hours later and found a place to stay. It was not a time of year that saw many tourists, so we were in luck. We explored some strawberry fields and the soils there for a while and went into town. There wasn't much to the town; it stretched only three blocks in each direction.

Every town in Venezuela has a plaza dedicated to its liberator, Simon Bolivar, where people spend afternoons and evenings. We spent the evening in Plaza Bolivar drinking hot chocolate and eating junk food. After talking and joking for an hour or so we got serious for a few moments.

The reason we'd gone to the town was not only explore it but to put it completely in God's hands. I spoke to the three brothers, basically telling them we were responsible for what God would do through us there. We spent the next thirty minutes praying over the town and thanking God for bringing us there.

That night we spoke with the one person in town in charge of transportation in and out of Piñango. Jeeps left to go to Eagle Peak, one in the morning and one in the afternoon.

We got up early the next morning to make sure we were on the jeep that was to leave at nine. Because transportation in Venezuela is not reliable at all, people know they have to be ahead of the game if they're going to get anywhere on time. But the morning jeep was full when we got there, so we got on the list for the afternoon jeep.

The delay afforded us an opportunity to explore the surrounding area a bit more. After breakfast we walked up the hill in the direction we'd come just the day before. We greeted people along the way and eventually made it to a small plot of lettuce. It took a while to locate the person who farmed there. We introduced ourselves, and I asked his permission to take a soil sample with me. He said it was perfectly fine, and I scooped up a few handfuls of soil, promising him I'd be back with the results.

When we got the results back, I sent them to Gorden, but to this day I haven't been back to share the results with that man. Thinking about that broken promise is a small reminder of my need to become better organized, something I need in all areas of my life. We were accomplishing many things as a team, but you can always sense when things are moving faster than you can keep up with.

We made it to the plaza with time to grab some empanadas and something to drink. The trip up to the peak and eventually home would be about four hours, so if we wanted to eat anything, we had to do it then. My chicken empanadas and malt soda were delicious.

The road to Eagle Peak was long and winding. The first part of the ascent was steep. Around a series of sharp bends we caught brief views of the western peaks and valleys in the distance. About halfway up the turns got less sharp and the incline less steep. Some wonderfully fertile farmland became visible, nestled between two rather large lakes. After this straightaway the bends returned and the temperature dropped.

The people walking on the side of the road were now wearing scarves and winter hats that covered their faces. We were only a few kilometers from the peak, and the sights became very familiar. The destination of the jeep was a town called Apartaderos. I never counted the time when I am up there as the sights are awesome.

From the peak we were actually going the opposite way from Timotes, but in Venezuela you take what you can get when it comes to transportation. After waiting for a few minutes in

Apartaderos, we got in another jeep leaving for Timotes, about forty-five minutes on clear roads.

Heading down the mountain, I noticed something I'd seen before but had never let sink in. As the landscape around the peak is one of absolute desolation, there is an almost visible line where the farmland ends as the elevation gets too high. It seems almost like a physical barrier beyond which crops can't grow. The farmers try to sneak past the line, but the crops just can't grow that high up.

The locals refer to everything around Timotes as the paramo. Many places surrounding Timotes are forests with heavy vegetation, although few people live up high on the peaks. Above the almost-physical barrier where only the frailejon plants live was what I always pictured as the real paramo. It seems though that what is paramo and what is not is open for discussion. The book definition is that of a high, desolate plain, but many who live here just refer to everything as paramo.

There is now a growing church in Piñango. The news, when Pastor Angel told me, was a huge blessing. The Lord had called my friend Maycol Sandoval to pastor this full-time ministry. A few months after our original visit a family made its way to the church in Timotes and showed interest in having some church members visit them. Eventually, a home church was formed there, and Maycol dedicated himself to those people. He went to them every time they needed him regardless of the distance. Maycol has extended the invitation to me to take me to the school in the clouds on his motorcycle, an invitation I will soon accept. He travels to Piñango every day on it, and his dedication motivates me to do more for others. Love is the ultimate motivator in the ministry. If you have love, you can succeed at whatever you do.

CHAPTER 21

More Dangers,
Toils, and Snares

Having decided to work independently in the mountains separate from any large organization, I was responsible for recruiting volunteers to help. I was working with Gorden in the full-time agricultural outreach, but I really wanted to get churches back home a chance to be involved with other projects in the area.

Allison, one of my friends and colleagues from my days in Caracas, wanted to come to Timotes on her vacation to assess needs and to see how she could help. We made plans to meet in Caracas and catch up with old friends and colleagues there first before flying back to Merida. It would mean I would have to leave Timotes two days before her arrival in the capital city. This was the perfect opportunity to utilize a voucher I had for a domestic flight.

Caracas is quite a ride from the Maiquetia airport, so it was best for us to meet at the airport and ride up the hill to the city together. I would need to take a bus to Maracaibo, get a flight, and meet my friend at the airport in Maiquetia. The plans seemed simple enough. Arriving safely in Maracaibo, I was also able to get a flight that would get me there with time to spare.

Like any domestic flight in the States, security is slightly less rigorous. To board any flight, however, a document check is necessary. My passport was good, but my six-month visa had expired the day before. I was detained and questioned by several uniformed men. They could have let me go on good faith that I would leave the country within the twenty-four-hour span all foreigners had by law to return to their native soil, but in the hours that followed I experienced the worst of humanity and the best of the God who loves me.

The immigration officers were not impressed with my mission work in the mountains. They kept asking me if I was carrying drugs. They saw I wasn't, having torn through my bags several times. The only reason they were interrogating me to this extent was simply because they could do it. They seemed to be enjoying it too. One of them said, "We don't believe you. Take off your clothes." I didn't have much choice in the matter as they were all armed. Watching these men enjoying themselves at my expense was very humiliating. They had me crouch, completely naked, and hop up and down. Their justification was to see if I was hiding drugs in any unusual places. The clear fact was that they did it to intimidate me and to have a good laugh. What seemed like several hours later they said to me, "We're done here, but you aren't." They threw me in a room and told me I'd be there until they could fully verify my reasons for being in their country.

The officers hadn't taken my cell phone, so I was able to send a text to Guillermo telling him I'd been detained at the airport in Maracaibo. His brother Javier, who lived close by, arrived minutes later, the quickest rescue ever. There were movies I'd seen in which the hero moved slower than Javier.

Jesus calls us his friends, and friends stand up for each other. They are never ashamed to say they are connected with you. Javier put himself in a very compromising position in standing up for me. He told them who I was, what I was doing in Venezuela, and took full responsibility for me until I could find an exiting flight.

As we drove to his home, he asked me if I was mad. I was obviously furious for what they'd done. He then said something I'll never forget. "You should be joyful! You suffered all that for Christ." It was the truth; we're all soldiers for him and should be willing to suffer anything for his sake. When we suffer things that we think are unfair or that we don't deserve to be going through, we should be joyful as we can see his love for us in everything.

That horrible experience taught me so much. Javier stood up for me though he could have easily denied knowing me to save his reputation. His decision put his reputation in jeopardy and possibly his business and his life. For that I will be forever grateful. I contemplated the words of an old hymn: "Stand up, stand up for Jesus."

Jesus calls me his friend. Was I willing to stand up for him as Javier did for me? As it turned out, I did stand up for him without knowing it. I wondered if it would have been in me to do that if the situation were graver and if standing up for Jesus risked my life. That was what was going through my head at that moment. Javier was a witness for me. Just like Jesus, he was my friend no matter what it may have cost him.

Another thing I was able to learn from being detained like that was that for those moments I had lost my freedom. Those men treated me the way they did simply because they were able to. It was a horrible display of arrogance and disrespect for another human being.

All those in sin are also in bondage just as I was during the time the immigration officers were disrespecting me. Gossip and criticism do not free people in bondage—action does. As Javier acted, we all need to act and befriend those lost in sin.

People in life will treat us badly at times just because they feel they can get away with it. This includes Christians and non-

Christians, but we have to forgive them all and move on. When fellow Christian believers treat me badly, I can't use that to justify any negative thoughts toward God. When we are truly filled with his presence we do not treat others poorly.

God has brought me through so many circumstances and so many dangers in my life. From running out of gas on the Colombian border to scuba diving in dangerous waters of the Caribbean to aiding in disaster relief efforts close to Caracas after a tremendous mudslide, countless times I was spared from serious harm. There were times when I failed to think straight and showed horrible judgment. There were times when I was clearly in the will of God, helping others. There were times where I should have sustained worse injuries or even died. The list seems endless, but God's love and protection is boundless. Even when we are in dangers, toils, and snares, his grace is amazing. It's wonderful to sing "Amazing Grace," and it's even more wonderful to experience it and to know it is real.

Rehabilitation

I locked my apartment door and marched into town. I set aside Mondays to shop for groceries and to catch up on personal projects. Even after having lived in Timotes for several months, it was still hard to believe how steep the hill was that got me into town. It amazed me that the farmers who lived up on this hill were able to make it up this steep incline even with no weight in the back of their vehicles. It is a great workout, so I shouldn't have grumbled. After all, the walk up the hill was worse than the descent. I made it into town in a few minutes and headed to the Chinese store.

Small supermarkets owned by Chinese entrepreneurs are all over Venezuela. The pleasant smell of cooking spices was overwhelming, but the man at the counter gave me a stern look that made me feel unwelcome. The prices are unbelievably low, so this was where I did most of my food shopping. I finished after several minutes and headed to the Internet café to quickly check e-mails before heading back up the hill. I was immediately met with the stench of body odor and alcohol.

A man, near fifty, was drunk at ten in the morning and blocking the sidewalk. He ran into me, but I was too saddened by what I saw to be annoyed. The scene was all too common in this small village; it has been tolerated for as long as my friends can remember. This problem affected a good majority of the families there, but very few had any clue how to make a difference.

The church in Timotes is now launching an effort to reach out to men and women affected by substance abuse. Studies have shown that recreational alcohol consumption by males in Latin America is on the rise, and we've noticed it in the mountains. In Timotes, alcoholism affects generally males, but whole families are destroyed when this happens. Alcohol use in the mountains can go beyond recreational when men don't have hope. The mountains can be very gloomy, and when some people here feel alone and hopeless, they turn to alcohol.

We're working on developing a rehab center. Having struggled with alcohol in the past myself, I realize that God has put me in the right place at the right time. Action on behalf of caring people in my life brought me out of my spiraling downfall and the hold that alcohol was starting to have on me. I couldn't in good conscience just have stood there and from a distance judged a drunk for his behavior; I felt called to help him.

I used to zigzag my way home from college parties much like the men I'd see every day in Timotes. I was able to find my way home to a warm bed and carry on when Monday came; these men, however, had nowhere to live, and their drinking was not for social reasons. They wanted to work but they couldn't. They found themselves completely dependent on alcohol. Someone helped me years ago, so I was more than happy to help someone else.

The young people in the church at Timotes have started a grassroots effort to bring men off the street to bathe them, feed them, and give them clean clothes. They have started the process of rehabilitation for these people who so desperately need it.

Whether they deal with people with substance abuse issues or not, the members of the church in Timotes realize it needs to be more proactive. Without compassionate action, people are powerless to change their own ways. Sin is powerful. When it becomes a physiological dependency, it makes it harder to quit and it becomes something that requires patience, love, and action to help someone overcome.

Our spiritual rehabilitation started when we accepted the fact that our dependency had to stop being on ourselves but on Christ alone. The process of starting the rehab center in the mountains requires action. The church in Timotes once again is inspiring me to act, and they are making me a part of it. The process is slow, but we continue to rely on the one who has called us to this work.

Working at extremely high altitudes taught me so much about what it means to adapt to new surroundings and how stubborn our bodies can be sometimes. When I first came to the mountains to live the thin air didn't bother me. But after being there a while, walking up and down hills to different farms and houses, it started to overwhelm me. The chilling cold in the mornings mixed with fatigue caused by thin air made it hard to get out of bed in the morning. It sapped all my energy and motivation. A hot coffee and an arepa with butter helped to get my day started, but for my first few visits here my productivity declined. It took a while to get accustomed to the thin air. Once my body adapted to the change, I was able to get more done.

Sin has the same effect on us. It chokes out the life and motivation we once had. It goes beyond just being something bad that God doesn't like. It becomes something that overtakes our life, and we are consumed by it. It also became clear to me that mere religion was not enough to change me.

Eliminating sin make us more productive, and it improves fellowship with everyone we have contact with. Just imagine how much quality time we miss with friends and with God because we spend most of it asking for forgiveness. If we disappointed others less, we would enjoy their company more. Prayer time would be better too since we wouldn't spend a majority of it just asking God to forgive us.

Over the years I've thought a lot about the difference between man's sinful nature and different addictions people suffer from. An addiction is a physical dependency, and I see how ineffective judging others with addictions can be. A simple act of faith can lead to pardon for our sins, but to help someone overcome an addiction we need to be patient. We need to help these people acclimate themselves to a new environment free of the substances they once relied on. Here in Timotes we have started at square one with our rehab center, and we have a lifetime of learning ahead.

I remember specific principles from my college years, including the concept of entropy, the quantitative measure of disorder in our universe. It is connected with the laws of thermodynamics that try to understand our planet and our universe as an evolved entity.

. The weathered rock on the mountaintops and the changing soils I studied were evidence of a changing environment, but faith is the measure Christians use to see how God is at work in the universe. I have seen God at work in the world around me over the past few years. He has put people in my life when it was in great disorder, and they were used to show me that my life has eternal purpose.

By God's grace alone I never followed the path of drinking long enough to become an alcoholic. Helping people fight addictions is still a cause dear to me, and it is a great blessing to see recovering alcoholics in different churches in the Andes who have been helped back to their feet. They have been renewed, and their thanksgiving is evident in their worship.

CHAPTER 23

El Alto

Having left the dirt footpath that we'd been on for hours, we finally reached a blacktop road leading to Timotes. My feet were not ready for the transition to a harder surface; they ached so much. I'd been walking in borrowed boots on rough terrain since before dawn. As there was a hint of rain in the air, the boys had lent me some waterproof boots, but they were a half size too small.

The hike we took that day was to Pueblo Llano, a three-hour hike to the peak, another half hour down to a flat spot that overlooked the town on the other side of the mountain, and a climb back to the peak and down again to Timotes. The trip by car to Pueblo Llano took close to four hours. This was the only place I'd ever been where you could get somewhere faster by foot than by car. We intended to complete this hike all in one day, and we were nearing the end of our eleven-hour journey.

From where I stood, the páramo was a vast highland with no end. Small communities and farms were hidden all over it, but as far up as we had been, there had not been many signs of life, only patches of grass, shrubs, and rocks. We saw an occasional bird, but only as we approached the road did we see tall trees.

About an hour earlier we'd passed El Muerto, an eerie landmark that consisted of a rock with a cross on it. Muerto in Spanish means "dead man." The landmark was a grave. The air was stale all over the mountain, but in that place it seemed heavier than normal. Apparently, several years earlier, an American tourist and his wife had been hiking up in those mountains and had gotten lost. The temperature dropped, as it normally does in the late afternoons, and they had died there from the cold.

Legend had it that the couple's family buried them under the rock we'd seen. The cross on top was the only memorial that remained. I began to think how sad it would be to die in the midst of such desolation, but then I started to think that it would be worse to live in desolation. It would be bad enough to live in an area surrounded by nothing, but I couldn't imagine anyone living his or her whole life without finding God's eternal purpose for him or her. That is the real reason I'd come there to live.

The peak we'd crossed to get down to the path to Pueblo Llano was El Alto, "high place." The El Alto passage was nearly twelve thousand feet high, and it was exhilarating to explore heights as high as that. The hike was a picture of my life's highs and lows. My life there had taken me to high places, and it had also taken me through despair and even close to death. I shared that day just as I shared my life, with friends. They had invited me to join them just as many people try to include friends to share moments in their lives. Invitations are open doors—we should be aware of them when they open, but so often we don't, and we thus miss out on great opportunities to share with others.

The boys used these opportunities to share with me, and such invitations allowed me to explore the awesome mountain scenery. I had been in Timotes for only a short time, but I already felt very close to these people. These boys, my new friends, wanted to spend time with me. They were my new neighbors but quickly became my new friends. Typical of people in the Andes, the boys were a bit shy and reserved when we first met, but sharing with them in a context familiar to them allowed me to get to know them very quickly.

The overcast sky was ominous. There was a late-afternoon chill in the air, and at the rate we were walking we wouldn't be home for another hour or so. My legs felt like rubber bands, but I found solace in the fact that the boys were also sore and tired and wanted to go home.

A while back Jhonattan had led us off the hiking trail and had gotten us lost. The main stream running down the mountain ran parallel to the hiking trail for most of the way down. Evaristo agreed to carry our heavy bags as Jhonattan fished. He was catching many fish, and in his haste he continued along the stream, leading us from the walking path. Evaristo and I started to worry as we saw the sun going down over the far peaks; the afternoon was quickly coming to an end. I was especially worried since I hadn't been that far up the mountain that late in the day before. My eyes remained fixed on El Alto as I tried to orient myself. Leaving the main path didn't seem as bad, though, when I remembered the three elements were still intact. There was someone to help carry the weight of the backpacks, someone to guide us back to the walking path, and friends who would not leave me.

Jhonattan loved adventure and spent little time at home. It was normal for him to do this, but not for the rest of us. We wanted to go home! It became necessary to persuade Jhonattan to leave the fishing for another day and start down the mountain.

Heading home on the trail, not too far from the stream where Jhonattan had been fishing, we saw footprints. They were so far off the trail, but we saw that others had occasion to come to this place so high up. I just hoped whoever those footprints belonged to were able to find their way back without getting lost any further.

The fear of being stranded was behind us, and we were back on track. Walking on a paved surface was not physically comforting, but it was a sign that we were getting closer to home. Lights from some farms in the distance became visible through a light mist that came in as afternoon transitioned into evening.

On this road was where I first met Mateo, the first person I met in Latin America whose name was the same as mine. That day, though, it didn't matter much to me if his name had been Billy, Fred, or Tom. My feet hurt so bad I was just thrilled when the boys told me that Mateo was heading home for the day and would give us a ride as he worked the farmland we had been walking through the previous several minutes. We were all in the back of the truck before they even introduced me to him.

A few months later Mateo gave up working on some of this farmland to work with our agricultural team as a missionary. This great sacrifice was a clear sign of his faith in God as this farmland fed his entire family. His missionary salary would barely cover his daily expenses. There must have been something strange in that mountain air or the water we were drinking for so many to leave their jobs to go into full-time missionary service.

The two Mateos, though, weren't the only ones giving up everything to follow God into the paramo; several followed soon after. Mateo and I had much more in common than just our names. Getting to know him as I do now and seeing how God has worked in his life and also in his family has been a great inspiration.

As the truck headed down the hill toward home, the boys enthusiastically pointed out the houses of Las Porqueras, a small farming community completely isolated by hills, hidden from the rest of the world. Some people who lived here had visited our church, and the pastor had sent one of the leaders up here, about a twenty-minute drive, to start a Bible study.

The boys were happy to tell me that the Bible study was now a small congregation that met weekly.

This community of just a few hundred people was one of several communities being penetrated by the love of God. There were more than a handful of new congregations popping up in these mountains, and a growing number of believers were becoming involved in ministry. My work in these mountains was primarily with the farmers, but with so many new areas similar to Las Porqueras to help out in, I was tending to the needs in these areas alongside different church leaders every day.

My Caracas friends had told me that the Venezuelan Andes were a sight to behold, but they never mentioned anything about its people. Getting to know them has been as much of a blessing for me as seeing the beauty of the surrounding mountains. It reminds me that God is the Creator and has made everything for us to enjoy along with him. This includes our relationships as much as it does the beauty of a sunset, climbing Mount Everest, or sailing the Pacific.

It is still a bit strange for me to see a ministry the size of ours here in the mountains. When people think of mountain country they often think of a very limited population, farm animals, and beautiful scenery. This was the case in Timotes. It was quite a contrast from the bumper-to-bumper traffic in Caracas and the sea of humanity one had to swim through every day to get on the subway. God is not interested in numbers, however; he has created all things for himself, and he wants to know all people, even those we take for granted sometimes as they are all precious to him.

I have worked in Venezuela as a missionary for close to ten years with different mission organizations; the personal path God led me on was similar to the hike we took that day, with many ups and downs.

Back on the blacktop, we were close once again to civilization. As we got closer to the homes and farms again, the bright colors of the vegetation reminded me of the colors on the golf course that had once stirred so much passion inside me—a place where I had been content to spend every day, never thinking I would ever want to leave. The bright green brought me back momentarily to the Tournament Players Club in Charlotte. There would be nothing better in my life than working at that place, or so I had thought. Back then my professional life was just starting, and I was moving closer to reaching my career goals with every passing day. So much had changed, and career goals mean little to nothing to me now. The only thing that matters to me is being a part of this Andean work and seeing it grow.

These fleeting thoughts of my old life are ended quickly as the chilly wind started to hit my face. The wind made it feel like January in New York. Riding in the back of a pickup truck was common here, and no one was complaining. The sun had set, and as we made a turn we saw the quiet and beautiful town lit up.

Just a few minutes later I was home. The metal door of my house creaked as I entered, and my feet hit the cold cement floor after my boots came off. I turned on the water heater so I could take a shower to clean off the mountain mud. It was only the dirt I wanted to wash off, not the day's memories. It had been one of the best days I'd spent in Timotes since arriving just a few months earlier.

I made it to the kitchen and lit the stove to make some tea and to warm me. In the bedroom I grabbed some clean clothes and a towel. The bedroom window was open; the view I enjoyed was of the town below and the other side of the valley.

The town at night was a gorgeous sight. Some of the all-night parties were quite loud, but that was how many here spent their nights. I don't spend nights like that anymore, but I remember when I did. Thinking back on my younger years, I realized how far I'd come to get here.

A light breeze came in the window, a more pleasant one than the one that had hit me on the mountain. I realized the magnitude of the miracle God has done. I'd seen places that day I would have otherwise seen only in books or documentaries. This creation is so immense and beautiful. The story of how I got there was equally impressive.

So much happened to take me from a life I thought was fulfilling to the point where I never wanted to leave the church family in Timotes, which I can't imagine living without. I'm blessed and honored to have experienced life here.

CHAPTER 24

A Valiant Rescue

Sometimes we have to go out of our way to get to where we are going. This was especially true in the weeks following massive flooding and mudslides just down the mountain from Timotes. Right around this time Pastor Angel and I needed to make a trip to Valera to pick up some important paperwork pertaining to my visa and to talk to a lawyer about the agricultural outreach program and how it could justify my getting a work visa to make it easier for me to continue living here. Pastor Angel was doing me a tremendous favor by sacrificing his day like this. But the way to Valera from Timotes, usually a straight shot down the main valley, was partially blocked by mud and debris. We tried to get to La Puerta to get to Valera, but that turned the normal one-hour trip into an all-day affair.

The bus kept stopping to wait for oncoming traffic to pass on the narrower-than-normal road. The North American in me started to come out, as I began to worry whether we'd make it to Valera in time for our appointment. It became more and more likely that we wouldn't as passengers were called on to move boulders aside for the bus to pass.

We came around a bend and saw a motorcycle tipped over in the middle of the road. The rider was nowhere to be seen. The bus stopped. We got off. We could hear gasps for breath and cries of pain. The rider had hit a bridge and had been thrown off his bike about thirty feet down. All we could see around him was blood. The situation was serious. We yelled to him that we could see him and that he should try to stay calm, but he just yelled louder because of the pain.

Just when the passengers were panicking and things were looking hopeless for the injured man, I saw Pastor Angel dart out of sight. He'd found a way down and wanted to comfort him. The man had several broken bones and was bleeding so badly that there was no way he would make it if something wasn't done right away. Someone called for help, but we were miles from the nearest hospital or clinic.

None of us had any medical background, but we realized that the bleeding needed to be stopped. We found some rags that we washed briefly in the nearby stream and applied to his more-serious wounds, but it didn't relieve his pain.

Pastor Angel, realizing that the man would bleed to death where he was, picked him up and carried him to the road. We flagged down a farmer with a flatbed truck and lifted the man onto the bed. We told the farmer to get him to the hospital in Timotes as fast as possible.

It took a while for us all to regain our composure, and no one really talked as the trip continued. What seemed like an inconvenient detour for us that day ended up saving a man's life. It's difficult to take the focus off our schedules and off the things we want to accomplish in a day, but it's necessary if we are really going to help others. We were all thinking about that man, hoping and praying that he got to the hospital in time. It was getting late, and the probability that we would make it to Valera that day was getting slimmer. But the road blockages became rarer, and they eventually stopped.

La Puerta is at a lower elevation than Timotes, but because the road climbed so much exiting Timotes we had more of a decent to get to La Puerta than just the difference in elevation between the two towns. No one was engaged in conversation. I was looking out the window. With every curve, the town would disappear for a while and then appear again, a little closer. A downhill straightaway gave us the sensation that we were in a plane that was landing. The scenario repeated itself until we made it to the last straightaway and eventually to the town's Plaza Bolivar.

When we finally made it to Guillermo's house, it was too late to think about making the forty-five minute trip to Valera. We were assured of a place to stay that night, and spending time with Guillermo was never dull, so we decided to get some rest and head to Valera in the morning.

Guillermo's wife, Elizabeth, made a great dinner, and we stayed up until almost two, talking and enjoying each other's company. We left the next morning before the rest of the family had gotten up. A small café next to the Catholic Church sold the best coffee in town. We had breakfast there, and while we waited for the bus to Valera, Pastor Angel seized the opportunity to teach me something. He was good at that. He told me that when we wake up in the morning it is not as important to be focused on what we wanted to accomplish that day but rather to be right where God wanted us to be able to impact someone else. An agenda is important, but people are much more important. Just like the detour we ran into that day, the road to friendship can be long, and our insecurities can be like detour signs. The ride to La Puerta had been a beautifully memorable one, and we learned a lot about ministry that day without ever expecting it.

On the way to Valera we discussed the man on the motorcycle. The pastor wanted to see him when we got back to Timotes. We talked about how far he had fallen. It looked so much farther from the bridge before Pastor Timotes went down to help him, not hesitating to run to the man's aid. We saw the motorcyclist later that week; he was still hospitalized but doing well.

Pastor Angel had taken part in a valiant rescue, and I had witnessed it. He was certainly brave to have acted so quickly. There are many people in trouble in this world. The first step in rescuing them is the most important. We just need to be willing to act.

CHAPTER 25

The View from Above

The truck came to a stop; we piled out of the back. Gregorio had been kind enough to take us halfway up the mountain again, but this time he was going to hike with us. The day was unseasonably warm and great for walking. We could have counted the clouds in the sky with one hand; it was a gorgeous day.

The Lighthouse group from Caracas was visiting again. The group had been to Timotes a few times before. These students took advantage of different vacation times during the year to partner with us in ministry. It was a blessing to me to see how well the church members in Timotes received the group from Caracas. The culture in the capital city is very foreign to the people in Timotes. If I hadn't experienced the cultures in both I would have never known. The teamwork they displayed was remarkable. The church members in Timotes shared their place with the newcomers from Caracas. They didn't act like experts on the mountain culture or look down on them for their lack of knowledge about it. This Lighthouse group had a different background, but everyone's goal was the same.

A new missionary couple had come to Caracas toward the end of Kathleen's term there to take over the work Kathleen and I had started. They formed a small congregation made up of students whom Roland, Kathleen, and I had worked with. The ministry was called Lighthouse, which functioned like a church but never formally became constituted as one.

My precious disciple Dagmar is married and a high school English teacher, a profession in which she will have much success. She showed dedication to her students in and outside the classroom. She openly shared about the God she'd come to know with many of them. Douglas, one of her students she has been sharing with, has become someone very special to Dagmar and me. He lives in Caracas, and he and I get along great. We share a love for music and baseball. He was a new believer in Christ, but that didn't stop him from becoming heavily involved in our work in the Andes.

I was happy to hear how Dagmar and her husband had become leaders in that ministry. It was an even bigger blessing to hear about Douglas and his spiritual growth. Douglas was becoming an important part of this group. In fact, I learned quite a bit of his story before I met him. I finally had that privilege in Timotes.

Finding out that Douglas was a Yankees fan was a bonus. The more important thing I found was his great love for people. He met Joaquin and immediately conversed with him. From there a lifelong friendship started. My two worlds had come together; my Caracas friends and my mountain friends formed inseparable bonds.

We did a very short excursion that day, but the group we had was rather large. There are many small peaks in Timotes, and each gives you a different view. The one we picked that day was ideal. Even with the head start it was still going to take us several hours to reach the top of one of the lower mountains.

We walked quickly, stopping occasionally to take pictures and explore the surroundings through occasional spaces in the bush. The dirt path we were on was wide enough for a truck, but it was strange to think any vehicles would ever pass us at such a high altitude. Very little was visible as we were surrounded by large bushes and small trees. The path was like a tunnel through vegetation on both sides, and only directly in front of us could we see the peaks far ahead. By the time we took the final curve, the trees and shrubs had vanished and just long grass encircled us. Making our way through the thick grass, we finally came to an unbelievable sight.

The view from this particular peak gave us a view of the entire town and the surrounding valley. The houses looked minuscule, and trucks looked like ants, not to mention people. We couldn't see any individuals down there. The quiet was eerie. There was just one audible whoosh, a mixture of all sounds from Timotes together.

Sitting up there with Douglas and the others, we looked at each other with smiles on our faces. We knew it was a special moment. There are times in life that are bigger than life, and one was the moment we enjoyed the view that day.

At that moment I began to think about Timotes and how it looked in God's eyes. In our mind's eye God is higher up than we are, yet he can be closer to us than anyone else. God is far above us and deserves to be, but he put himself on our level when he sent his Son to live among us.

Having Timotes in my sight for those moments just magnified the truth I had known about God's love. It was for every speck we saw down there and every speck all over the globe. It made no sense to me how something so small could mean so much to God. It also made no sense to me how we don't try hard enough to put ourselves on the level of other people as Jesus had. We always want to be a little higher than the other person; we do this to make ourselves feel more important.

The Great Commission is the command Christ gives us to share his truth with all nations. With a command that great, there is no room for jealousy or competition. As a body of believers, we have such a scope of talents and gifts to offer

God. Instead of using them to the maximum, we tend to try to one-up each other. Recognition on earth is not the goal; it's finishing the jobs we've been given.

It really doesn't matter if I'm the one to start a Bible study or the first to invite someone to church. The most important thing is that I am plugged into the ministry I need to be plugged into. There is something unique for every one of us, and we can be used in special ways.

Observing the church members in Timotes, I have seen that more can be accomplished when we do not try to do what others are better gifted at doing. Years of experience and closeness has taught them that working together will give them much better results than trying to outdo each other.

New faces appeared in the Timotes church every Sunday. Sometimes we met families who lived halfway up the mountain. We would at times take advantage of the locations of some of their homes to have special church services. The Lighthouse group came especially for a service with a family who had opened their doors to the church. We brought a video about the life of Jim Elliot to show to the youth. Jim Elliot was a fearless young missionary who had lost his life in the jungles of Ecuador, and his story touched the young hearts that experienced his story that night. These homes overlooked everything, and the entire town could hear the worship with the booming sound system we'd set up.

The most vivid of memories from those services was how Pastor Angel used the location to spread God's Word. Some talk about God constantly without really impacting us, but a man with a clear message and a heart full of love talking about God can be extremely powerful. I remember him shouting from those hilltops with a megaphone, just telling the population of Timotes about what he had experienced of God's love and how it could lift them out of whatever they were going through.

The sound echoed throughout the valley. People heard that message and had no choice but to contemplate the truth they'd just heard. The walk to this particular home was straight up the steepest hill I'd ever seen. It was such a relief getting there after the long walk, and most people went in their trucks or on motorcycles. The view from that spot is breathtaking, but the view I had of God that night was heavenly. The congregation of Timotes defied gravity on so many occasions. They began to regularly meet at that home for special services, carrying the heavy sound equipment there. They lifted the whole weight of Timotes up that hill as well, carrying their burdens in prayer.

The action defies what humans would consider possible, just as pulling a heavy weight uphill does. We go downhill faster, and people are happy to help us to move downward with a kick. A lot of times kind words are harder to find than hurtful ones. Only love can pull someone uphill and out of rebellion. I was there in Timotes because someone had done that for me.

Love puts us on the same level. The people up on the hill were from a culture the complete opposite of mine. The height of their small community kept them a bit isolated from the rest of town. They physically looked down on the town, but in reality they looked down on no one; they sought to be servants to those different from them. Their love for me put us on the same level.

I've been treated like an inferior in the past, and it's no fun. We miss opportunities to share with new people when we look down on them because of prejudices. Those who make less money or have less education are looked down on. They are like the specks we saw so far down from that peak in Timotes. The view from above is extraordinarily beautiful, but it is greater when we get on the same level as those around us.

You don't need to be on top of a mountain to be close to God. As I stood on that peak with the group that day we all hiked up there, I was able to make out the figure of the new church building in the middle of town. It looked so far away, yet we all remembered feeling his presence the night before during a worship service. We felt his presence on top of that mountain too as we enjoyed the view. If his presence was way down there and dwelling within us way up on the mountain, that means he is everywhere.

He is everywhere—Mexico, Haiti, and New York.

I took Richard's advice about going wherever God needed me most. The answer to my prayers about my permanent work visa was not the one I had hoped to get. It didn't look like I would ever live permanently in Venezuela. A few trips to Mexico with Gordon afforded me the opportunity to leave Venezuela for a while so as not to overstay my visa. I was traveling a lot, but it meant I'd be spending time away from Timotes, and that made me sad.

CHAPTER 26

Home Again

Things in life seem to come full circle. I was using the experience and knowledge about plants I'd gained on golf courses, the agricultural ministry was an education in itself, and I was getting a lot of chances to exercise my newfound knowledge. Everything was coming back to where it had started, but the agricultural ministry was branching to so many new areas. Gorden's work was growing in leaps and bounds. Invitations came from other cities in Venezuela as well as other countries for Gorden to go and share his knowledge in the form of soil seminars. We made a few trips as a team to Mexico, and Gorden went by himself to Haiti. Gorden had a message that farmers around the world must hear. They were poisoning their lands with harsh chemicals, and it was important that they learned how to grow more-organic crops.

I was happy to see this ministry grow. Gorden was teaching me not just about farming but about how to walk with God. There was also a feeling within me that my call was to the people here in Timotes, not Mexico and not Haiti. There was one more trip I took with Gorden to Mexico, but it was my last.

The hardest decision I had to make in my young life was to leave this team and go home to New York. It has been a few years since I'd seen my family and friends there, although we'd swap occasional e-mails. My relationship with Gorden has never been the same, and I miss him. One day, after returning from that trip to Mexico with Gorden, I went to stay at his house for a few days. I remember very little of the events leading up to this moment. I was showering in his guest bathroom, and as I was starting to get dressed I passed out. It took a few minutes for me to wake up and realize what had happened. Gorden took me immediately to the doctor. They ran several blood tests but found nothing wrong.

A few weeks later we went to see another doctor, who suggested that my body had been overrun by parasites that had been in my system for many years and that certain foods I had been eating recently made the condition unbearable for me. After follow-ups with several other doctors, it seemed that the diagnosis was accurate, and it was a condition that I would have for several years after. It was a slow process, but following a strict diet for a few years helped me eliminate them almost one hundred percent from my body.

Working and spending so much time together, Gorden and I had developed a relationship far beyond a simple working relationship, and I knew he cared deeply for me. He said the best thing for me to do was to just go back to New York to get my illness under control. I did just that, but in the months to come I would still make a few trips to Timotes; it was impossible at that point to keep me away.

While I was home I made the decision to take a class that would raise my awful college grade point average, something I needed to do to get accepted into seminary. I took any job I could find in New York for the next three years, from courtroom interpreter to phone representative and even substitute teacher. I did whatever was necessary to pay rent and tuition. When the letter came that I had been accepted to seminary, it was a feeling that things were finally moving forward after so much academic disappointment.

During the time spent at home, I was able to spend time with my grandmother for the first time in years. She could no longer cook for herself, so I'd bring meals to her on occasion. Those moments taught me a lot about servanthood, that serving others is a blessing far beyond being served by others.

My grandma and I would sit on her porch in the summer and watch the boats on the Hudson. She loved that river, and it was tough to get her off the porch at night. She didn't live alone, but she spent a lot of time alone. She cherished the times when people would visit; she loved having company even when she was younger. Sitting and talking with her were moments of pure fellowship, an inkling of the fellowship God desires to have with each of us.

She was the only one of my grandparents I ever got to share with. My mother's parents had died before I was born. I remember my grandma taking trips with us to Disney World. My father converted the back of his then-new pickup into a sleeping space for us. My sister and I rode back there with her. Confined spaces and young children will test the patience of the most loving grandparent.

We spent Christmas evenings at grandma's house, opening gifts and drinking eggnog. We were close because we lived close to her, but as I got older and different responsibilities took me out of town I wasn't able to see her as much. This picture is almost identical to my walk with God: close at the beginning, a time when I moved away, and finally enjoying close fellowship again as I tend to her needs.

I enrolled in seminary after such a long time on the mission field and moved into an apartment in Albany. I had to work two jobs to pay for it, but I also had some time left over to study. My plan was to stay there until I finished school. The apartment, in an up-and-coming neighborhood, was beautiful. I rarely use the word "perfect" since I have come to the knowledge that only God is perfect, but my apartment was the closest thing to perfect I'd enjoyed in a long time.

Albany was about thirty minutes from the town my grandmother lived in. I went down on weekends to check on her, but during the week it was just not possible. She was in good hands during the week; my mother and father were there as well as the family friend who stayed with her. It was still an obligation I felt important to keep, and I tried to get there as much as I could.

This trip home from Venezuela would prove to be permanent, and with the move came many challenges. In Timotes I'd been surrounded by people of like faith every day. In New York my faith had to be strong. I was back to a nine-to-five job, and coworkers were inviting me to share with them outside work.

Just like the prayer life I had developed over the years, sharing with friends was usually unplanned and spontaneous but wonderful. Spending time with nonbelievers should in no way be connected to temptation. It is an excuse we use to not get to know others or spend time with them.

After finishing two semesters at school it was time to visit Venezuela. I'd moved back with my parents to help take care of my grandmother and to free up rent money to finish school quicker. The decision also freed up some money to travel a few times a year to Timotes.

It was important to be present in Timotes at that juncture; it was a pivotal time of growth for the church. Returning there, I saw that they had five new missions they wanted to form into churches.

There was a lot of work ahead for them, but things were moving forward. Things were moving forward for me too, albeit very slowly, but they never stopped moving. I was recovering from my illness, had some credits under my belt in seminary, and I was making enough money at the time to pay for everything. Timotes and my mountain family were far away, but God was allowing me to stay connected to the work there. In my times of prayer I thanked God for having them in my life.

Just ten years earlier my work on the golf course had been the most significant thing in my life, and I wouldn't have exchanged it for anything. The golf course had been my heaven, and I found myself clinging to it as if there would be nothing better for me. I thought it was enough for me, just like my eternal security was enough for so many years. In the States and in Venezuela I've seen many people in church cling to the fact that they are saved and are going to heaven. That is something to rejoice about and something I would never make light of, since Christ died so we can enjoy eternity with him.

God has shown me how important my life on earth is to him. Having come so close to death many times, I now see that we have a limited window to make an impact on our world. It is important to him that we make use every moment we have.

The realization that home would be wherever God's will was led me to concentrate on others and to help them. This brought more and more satisfaction and enjoyment to my life. Leaving home and starting a new journey in the mountains of Venezuela showed me what abundant life really is, Christ's love filling me. I could be in New Jersey, New York, or even New Guinea. It doesn't matter. The abundant life Christ gives us is to be shared with others; there is enough to go around. Learning this and also living it leads us all back home.

Joaquin took a trip with me to Maracaibo before I left the country for the last time as a permanent member of the ministry team in the mountains. We were there for only a few days, but it was enough for him to make quite an impact. We went to a birthday party in Cabimas where he was as much the center of attention as the girl having the birthday. This was the first time Joaquin had ever been out of the Andes and in a city, but he was received in love and made many friends. The love that received him made the difference.

This was also Joaquin's first experience with modern technology. He was amazed at the displays at the mall we went to, and he stumbled getting on an escalator. We still have a chuckle about that; Joaquin takes it in good fun and lets out a belly laugh. But he was excited to experience new things. As someone who had also been in a new environment, I could identify with Joaquin, and it brought us closer together.

The most memorable part of the trip was the Saturday night we attended a youth service in Cabimas. On his first visit to the First Baptist Church of Cabimas, or La Primera as it was affectionately known there, he asked the musicians if he could practice a song with them. They practiced the song for five minutes, but the musicians told him there was no time at the service that night to sing it; he would have to sing during the Sunday service.

At the time of our trip, La Primera had about three times the attendance of the church in Timotes. (That's not the case anymore, as the church in Timotes has exploded in size.) I thought the large congregation would affect his singing, but it didn't affect it at all; he left everyone with hands raised in worship and crying.

Joaquin doesn't know what an inspiration he has been to me. Several weeks later I returned to Cabimas and sang a song in English. This enthusiasm was contagious, and it was not staying just in Timotes. Joaquin's song was the first of many examples of missionaries from the mountains to be used of God in larger cities. This work didn't all start in Timotes, but it took off exponentially from there.

CHAPTER 27

Generosity

Patricia walked up to my cubicle and waited until I finished my phone call. She handed me a piece of paper and said, "God Bless You." She smiled and walked away. The paper she handed me was a very generous check.

We'd been coworkers for a very short time, but this was a job I'd worked off and on for a few years. I was utilized as a bilingual, spending my days there translating recordings from Spanish to English and also interviewing customers in their native Spanish language. Management was very flexible with my travel to Venezuela and allowed me to take time off when I needed it. It was a great job, as I got to use my Spanish and got along great with everyone there. I worked there more and more as my trips got shorter and the time between them got longer.

I had shared very little about my ministry in Venezuela with Patricia. Our conversations were mostly about our jobs and lifting each other up during long work days with some light humor or funny stories. I knew she and her husband were ministering in a church nearby, and she knew I traveled a lot to Venezuela, but we never got to the specifics of my work there, so it was a surprise to me when she told me she wanted to help me financially. I was convinced that her generosity would connect her directly with the people in the mountains, but something I learned about her more than confirmed this conviction. When she told me, the news blew me away.

One day I came into work in the late afternoon to start my normal shift. We began talking, and I noticed she was reading a textbook. To make polite conversation with her I quipped, "Looks like someone is heading back to school." She responded in a very matter-of-fact manner, almost as if she were talking to a complete stranger. "Yes, I've decided to go back to school to become a substance abuse counselor." In the kingdom of God there are no coincidences.

This was a time of transition for me from full-time international ministry to a day-to-day working routine in the States. Life in the States was tough on me as I worked part time and traveled every few months to Venezuela. This was an extremely trying time for me, but I was not about to turn back. I was never the betting type, but as far as the Andean work was concerned I was pushing all my chips to the center of the table. God would get me through this time of uncertainty just as he had done many times before.

The period of transition lasted about two years. My all-out commitment to the Andean work showed my unfettered faith in God. I trusted him for every breath, every meal, and every dime as I made my short trips during those two years. It was a price that had to be paid, but I am glad I did it. The churches in the mountains were going through some very trying times. I felt the need to be physically present with them and so went there two or three times a year. This, I hoped, gave them the assurance they were not alone through all of this.

There were things under the surface that were happening that most of my friends and family couldn't see. My day-to-day life in New York was something everyone could see. My desire to continue following God in the mountains wasn't an outwardly obvious thing, so it became something no one understood. They couldn't understand that God was calling me to help people they'd never met, and it was hard for me to help them feel connected to the work.

Merely working in the States and sending money to Timotes would not have led me to the connection I now have with my church family in the mountains. The hardships and the things we suffered together brought us closer. Some changes in my life are in motion now to increase my income and invest it better, but now I have the knowledge of what really has value and the price that has to be paid for it.

Patricia always asked me when I would be traveling again. Without fail she would come by my desk and drop off a check just a few days before my trip, which was badly needed at the time. Patricia gave to me because she loved me, and, more important, loved God. She also did it because she'd worked hard at her job and the money was available to her to be able to give it. Patricia was a living example of wholehearted giving, which begins with us being responsible first with what God gives us with through our labor.

Patricia's generosity showed me that she believed in me and that the work I was doing in Venezuela connected her to the people there. She didn't seek to get anything in return for her giving; she just did it because God put it in her heart to help me. It seems so simple, but it was something I had to learn: money is necessary. I learned when and how to spend money. There was nothing wrong with accepting a check from someone who wanted to be part of the work. I also learned that I couldn't just live my life with my hand out, expecting people to fund my work. Nor could I work endless hours to make a bunch of money just to hoard it for myself.

Sometimes we need to have the perspective of what our whole life will look like when we are done living, not just what it looks like during the weeks and months we happen to be struggling to survive. During those times I probably appeared to be stingy and selfish. God was not concerned about how people saw me; he was fixing my eyes on a vision that was consuming my whole life.

The question everyone asks you in life is "What do you do?" There were times when I didn't have an answer to that question, and things would get awkward. Most people approaching forty have a solid answer to that question. Many don't expect a person of my age to have just a part-time job at a bakery or a school. Some people weren't impressed with my work in South America because it didn't pay a six-figure salary. It took me a few months to realize I didn't need a title to affirm my purpose in life. I remembered a time just a few months prior when the deacons from the church in Timotes had laid hands on me and prayed for me, thus commissioning me to work with them.

My plan all along was to go home, start seminary, and stay home until school was done. Some grave circumstances surrounding the ministry in the mountains made it necessary for me to travel and to spend one-on-one time with pastors and missionaries to verbalize plans for our future. I brought their message back with me to ask for support from churches in the States.

My jobs in New York were allowing me to pay down debt, pay for school, and pay rent. For the first time in years I had a stable life. I gave it up to be with my brothers and sisters in the mountains when they felt they had no one else. The price is paid in our sacrifice, not in what we spend of our earnings.

Spending time with friends who had accumulated material possessions over the years was a big temptation. Many of them had big houses, classy boats, and fancy clothes. They would buy me nice gifts on my birthday and Christmas, and I felt bad when I couldn't return the favor. These friends had learned that success in business is found by not giving anything away. They had been responsible in their professions, so they could demonstrate generosity to me, and others.

It was hard at times not to be overcome with jealousy. I wanted so badly to have a lifestyle like theirs, but it became clear to me that God had allowed me to live extraordinary experiences and still wanted to use me. Yet another lesson was being taught to me, but I wasn't yet seeing it. Once I learned it, my efforts in the mountains would be more productive.

My experiences over the past few years had already taught me the lesson, but sometimes I am slow to catch on. So, until I learned this lesson I had to decide. Would I concentrate on just making a financially comfortable life for myself, or would I continue to travel to Timotes and spend all my money on trips?

During this time I was relying on help from different people, but I had to be careful. So many times we flock to people with money and let them control us. That would be the wrong kind of sacrifice because it wouldn't bring us closer to God. It ends up that we submit to them for what their money can do for us or for our work.

These years of struggle taught me that people are impressed with someone earning a hefty wage. It's hard to gravitate toward someone who is reduced to returning bottles and cans to raise gas money, as I was at one point. This reality affected me not because I wanted to been seen in a different light by friends and family but for another reason. My lack of money during that time kept me from giving like I wanted to. It was tough during those months to take more than I was giving. My trips became so expensive that I was not able to continue tithing in my church. It was tough to attend church knowing I was not honoring God or my commitment to my local congregation. Speaking engagements had me traveling so much that I had to discontinue my membership; faithfulness in attendance is important. Stewardship of time and riches are both important to God.

Tithing is something God asks us to do through our churches. It is the giving of the first fruits of what he gives us and should be done in faith. Tithing is not at all comparable to paying dues to become a member but something that comes along with church membership. So, not continuing to attend church was never an option, but God was setting my eyes on Timotes, although I was physically far from that church.

Before leaving to come back to the States I was a tithing member of the church in Timotes. Because the support I was receiving during that time was coming in dollars, my tithe was considerably high due to the exchange rate between U.S. dollars and Venezuelan bolivares. But the amount I was able to give did not exempt me from submitting to leadership, nor did it buy me extra influence. It helped me trust God more and more as I saw the money we were giving collectively as a church go to supporting missionaries and growing our rehab center.

Knowing I would not be back in Venezuela to live for at least a few years, my commitment as a member could not continue. I had to discontinue my membership, moving so far away, but I still gave offerings when I visited.

We should give above and beyond the few dollars we put in the offering plate or in the donation jar at the supermarket. Our whole life should be a life of giving. There is no limit of the needs to be met in this world.

My crises of generosity led me to understand that people see what's on the surface but that God sees our hearts. My offerings were comparable to the mites the widow from the Bible story gave. I learned that the amount we give is not important because God owns it all anyway. He wants all of us. Considering my past failures at the time he called me, it was still hard to believe that he had called me! I myself could have been seen just like that widow's mite. I didn't think I had much value, but God's exchange rate is always favorable.

True generosity comes when you decide to give wholeheartedly to something without questioning it. Prayer and the resulting peace will confirm whether it is a good cause you're giving to. Sometimes we're not as generous as we think; generosity is not just giving more than we receive. I've learned that not spending money at all or being cheap does not make you a good steward, but giving large offerings doesn't make you a saint. God is not asking us to give just our money and possessions; he is asking us to give ourselves away.

CHAPTER 28

The Ascent to the Páramo

The bus terminal in Valera was buzzing. Taxi drivers were yelling to anyone who would listen, making their destinations known. The chorus of *colectores* was audible: "Maracaibo! Maracaibo!" "Valencia directo! Valencia Valencia!" They were shouting the destinations of the buses to fill each one. Valera, the largest city to the north of the paramo, is like most cities in Venezuela, fast-paced and loud. It was a scene that would horrify any American traveler, but I was used to it. I was guiding Douglas through it.

It had been eighteen months since I'd been to Venezuela. This was the longest stretch I had gone without traveling since my feet first hit the tarmac in Maracaibo and this labor of love in Venezuela started so many years ago. It was mid-December, Douglas and I were going to Timotes to spend Christmas with our precious friends there and possibly even welcome in the New Year with them.

Whenever I was in the Valera terminal, I made sure to visit my good friend Jeremiah. He lived in Timotes but had a stand in the terminal where he sold snacks and other items. After chatting with him for a few minutes, I treated Douglas to some snacks for the ride up the hill, and we continued our walk to the bus. Douglas reminded me that junk food was no good for us, but the Ruffles potato chips that Jeremiah sells are always very good, especially with a soda.

As we made our way through the hustle and bustle of the colectores and taxi drivers, we came to a strip of smaller buses for local routes only. It was there that I found a bus to Timotes. Here, though, instead of having destinations shouted in my ear, I had to ask the driver where he was going. The contrast in culture was so evident. The passengers were sitting on a bench and almost whispering to each other. Passengers from any other part of Venezuela were a lot louder.

We left Valera shortly after and headed up the mountain. A soft *vallenato*, music from Colombia, played at a low volume, as opposed to the *reggeton* that would be blasting at full volume if we were in Caracas or Maracaibo.

Another cultural difference became evident. Douglas and I had shared many bus rides in Caracas and had to shout at each other to have a conversation. But on our bus no one was talking, and Douglas put on headphones to relax a little.

The first few curves in the road didn't take us far out of Valera, and for the next several kilometers an urban environment mixed with trees and streams. The ascent to the north side of this mountain is much steeper than on the Mérida side. The climate changes quickly, and there is one curve in particular where you can notice a sharp drop in temperature. We went from seeing kids in shorts and sandals to seeing people in light jackets in a matter of minutes.

My mind drifted, and I began thinking of everything God has taught me in Venezuela. I thought about the many congregations I'd seen formed. New congregations were popping up all over, but it was not anything I wanted to take for granted. The church-planting process is a marvelous one, and God's leadership must be respected each time a new work is started. There were experiences I had to live and learn from before I got to this point.

Douglas was quietly listening to his music on his headphones. We chatted occasionally along the way, but for the most part I continued thinking about things. It amazed me that I was there, and I sat in quiet reflection. It was hard for me to learn that regardless of where you were in life God was constantly preparing you for the next step in his grand plan. My short time in Caracas had been a process of learning what a healthy church needs to grow and replicate itself throughout the world. It was after living these experiences that I felt ready to join this church-planting movement in the mountains.

I looked out of the bus and saw the walking bridges over a *quebrada*, or stream, that runs down to Lake Maracaibo from the top of the mountains. The stream, quiet and harmless then, sounds like Niagara Falls even up in Timotes when the rains fill it to capacity in the winter, when it rains every day.

These walking bridges, made by hand, are the only way to get to the homes on the other side of the water. These bridges remind me of the challenges that faced us as we shared with these people. We were still traveling in a rural area outside of Valera, and though the homes were scarce, it didn't make them less valuable.

We soon passed a spot with a name inspired by this small river. La Quebrada de Cuevas, about halfway between Valera and Timotes, is made up mostly of roadside hamburger stands and restaurants selling roast chicken. The bus let a few people off. There is no church in La Quebrada de Cuevas, but we hope there will be one soon. We have been moving down the mountain from Timotes toward this town in our effort to plant churches.

Many times as I ride these buses I think about the people I see. It makes me sad that they may not know the very reason they are alive or what they are capable of accomplishing. Philippians 4:13 says that "I can do all things through Christ who strengtheneth me." This passage pertains just as much to the Christian who has been in church for twenty years as it does for the recovering drug addict or former prostitute with very little time in church.

We have had occasion to share with people on these buses and have seen that just like in many places in the world, people in these mountains have formed opinions on religion as nothing more than a set of rules. Many people are afraid of churches and don't want to visit them because they feel the focus there is placed on what they can't do. This verse in Philippians does not use the words "can not" but one single word, "can."

I nudged Douglas; the girl behind us had been looking at him, trying to get his attention. They began talking, a conversation that led to an exchange of phone numbers. It was not typical to meet such an outgoing person here. I joked with him and told him to stop flirting with the locals, and he laughed. "Besides," I said, "we have a long way to go before we get to Timotes."

For most of the trip up the mountainside the quebrada is to the left of the bus. We reached the bridge in front of the entrance to Jajo, where we were starting a church. The level of the road rises here, putting the stream out of sight for a few miles. I looked up and saw the El Horno church, a congregation I had the honor of pastoring for a few months until another missionary took over. It was way off to the right of the bus, up high, hanging off a cliff. From where we were it looked as if it would fall on us.

It's common for traffic to stop for slight reasons, perhaps a dog in the road or a stalled vehicle ahead; we found ourselves stopped for a few extra minutes, which allowed me to admire the El Horno church. I asked Douglas if he could see it. He told me that he could but that he'd never visited it. I told him the story about how the church started. His head tilted up and his eyes widened as he listened to the story of Antonio and Maria and the church. He had not heard many stories of my time in Caracas. Dagmar used to tell him stories about me, but he'd never heard my accounts firsthand. He was curious to know more about Enoch, someone Dagmar talked about a lot. I started to tell him the story of Enoch and how we'd met. I also told him about my trip to Machu Picchu and how one of my greatest disappointments was not having pictures of that place.

"Well, you have your memories," he said. He was right, I had my memories, and they still teach me a lot. As Pastor Angel and Guillermo had done so many times, I related my experiences to Douglas to try to teach him something.

"Having Enoch with me in Caracas was a tremendous help," I told Douglas. "Preparing for a permanent visitor to come reside with me was certainly a start to learning how to have a successful ministry. Once I learned it was impossible to do it alone, the work actually became easier. The Holy Spirit has become the permanent visitor that has changed me the most."

"And hiking the Inca Trail was tough," I continued. "We were glad to have a guide and help with our bags. I know I couldn't have made it without Kevin either." Recognizing and appreciating the importance of the three spiritual elements also helped me understand how a church as a living body remains healthy and grows. "It is pretty cool how the Trinity was illustrated to me during that trip."

Seeing this paramo from another angle was interesting. It was the first time I'd come this way because this road gets covered by landslides quite a bit. It was still great to ride through some of these small towns we were now working in. Several passengers had gotten off at Jajo, so the bus was lighter, but it still had its steepest incline to climb.

A few minutes later we passed through the small settlement of San Francisco, where a church had also been started. Douglas yelled out, "Hey! I've been there!" He was remembering one of the first trips the Lighthouse group had taken. They had helped us visit and invite people in the area to an activity for kids. The youth from the church in Timotes put on a puppet show for the community, one of the first steps in building the congregation that still functioned there.

Soon the bus made another stop, one I knew well, La Mesa de Esnujaque. A rather large church has been there for years and was working with us in the agricultural ministry. These efforts have been very fruitful in some of the hidden farming populations in this area. It is so important for Christians to believe in each other as they work toward the common goal.

A lot of people got on and off the bus there. I started to think about the church in La Mesa and how I hadn't been to visit them in a while. This church existed many years before our church planting began, they were still willing and eager to work alongside us. I also thought about what I had learned about teamwork from my friend Angel. I remembered when one day a young man from the church made a comment that God believed in us. Pastor Angel quickly scolded the young man and included me in this exhortation although I hadn't made the comment; he wanted to make sure his point was clear to me too. "God does not believe in man; he loves man. The difference is significant. It is impossible for God to believe in man if apart from him we can do nothing." His words were clear and to the point. We all understood after he was done speaking. I chalked that up to another lesson learned; if God's presence is in a fellow believer, then we must also believe that God is at work in his or her life. We need to believe in each other and trust that God is working out his plan in the lives of Christians around us.

At a stop near La Mesa is an overhead walking bridge I never saw used. Taxis and buses drop people off in front of La Mesa entrance, and instead of utilizing the overpass that could make it safer, they just run across the busy road.

We continued our journey, and a very sharp curve was next for our driver. The double curve took us past the Y intersection, and we were on the final straightaway that led to Timotes. That intersection always brings back memories, as this was where I had to spend a whole afternoon waiting for a taxi to take me to La Puerta so many years earlier. At that intersection one road took me to a man who helped form me into the missionary I am today. The road up the mountain led to the man who is now mentoring me as the church-planting efforts intensify here. I learned what leadership is from the two. They have shown me that a true leader in church gains influence by showing love and understanding to others. A leader in church is also placed there by God and is given automatic authority. There is no process they need to go through to earn respect; their influence should be a product of their love for others.

In the final straightaway the road gets a bit steeper. Another bridge brings us over the quebrada for a last time. For the rest of the trip, and for the whole extent of Timotes if you are traveling that far, the stream runs to the left of town as you look toward Eagle Peak. A sign comes into view that welcomes travelers to Mérida, a state with very few churches until recently. The booming church in Timotes is an example to many.

Farmland is visible in the distance to the left, but as we get closer to Timotes some roadside homes block the view. At that point you can see houses close to roads that go to smaller villages on the side of the mountain. Where there are none of these roads we have a clear view of acres and acres of farmland in the distance.

The valley widens after a sharp curve and there is land on the far side of the stream, which hugs the mountain most of the way up. Close to Timotes, the farmers can be a little more liberal with where they plant; they don't have to be as creative as they have more flat land to enjoy. Farms with more land are run very well, with several employees working on them. They are almost like small corporations. "See that farm over there?", I ask Douglas. "We visited it often when I lived here, it does very well." A church is similar to a business in its organization, but the leadership structure needs to be distinct or it will not flourish.

"Just like the work on these farms, a fruitful ministry involves everyone and places value on others", I continue. " So many times we base our holiness on our opinions. An effective church bridges the gap between the community and God." The true essence of a church, and this became very clear to me during my preparation as a missionary, is in its unity.

There have been minor conflicts during our efforts in Timotes. The church members here recognize that the men of God behind their pulpits have been placed there by God and have been given authority by him. The churches here had unwavering respect and dedication to their pastors. Not afraid that my preaching will bore Douglas, I add "Submitting to a pastor's authority may be the wisest thing I have done in my entire ministry." The words of Jesus are so clear when he says "all authority hath been given to me." The key word in this passage is "given." Some Christians assume authority and base it on the amount of time they have been attending church or the amount of money they give. Obedience to authority is what kept me alive in such a dangerous country, and it is what continues to grow God's kingdom in many churches around the world.

God had certainly showed me where I fit in as far as his plans for me and the church. I had not earned the right to be used by God the way I was, but my years in Venezuela were a testimony of a change and of God's presence in my life. My days in Caracas were a preparation for something that God had preordained here in the Andes.

The bus shook and jolted us as it shifted gears, preparing for the steepest part of the ascent. The bus continued for a few more minutes before it reached civilization again. Houses and people became more numerous, and we soon passed through the tollbooth in Chiquiao that had not been charging tolls as far back as I'd been here. After a few minutes the road leveled out, and stops became more frequent. We had made it to Timotes.

I asked the driver to drop us off in Los Llanitos, just below town.

When we arrived at the pastor's house, the family prepared a quick cup of coffee. The pastor pulled me into his makeshift office and stressed the importance of what he was going to preach that night at the midweek worship service and the profound desire he had to see this church follow the great vision God had given him. It was there that I knew the church in Timotes was going to be a healthy church and would flourish; they had been given a great leader who cared deeply for them and had been given a great vision with which to lead the flock.

Less than a handful of years ago, I was someone with a very superficial knowledge of spiritual things. God's love has penetrated even my stubborn being and I am now mentoring Douglas in our continued effort to bring light to places that are as dark and desolate as my heart once was. As we left the pastor's office and headed out of the house, I knew my ascent to the páramo was complete.

CHAPTER 29

The True Beauty
of the Páramo

The Thursday-night leadership meeting with Pastor Angel wrapped up early. We were surprised to be out so early as we were used to long, passionate discussions about how to reach the Andean community that were followed by a time of prayer. This meeting was full of the same passion, just not as long. All in all I was glad Douglas got to see how Pastor Angel developed his leaders.

There were no other places we had to be that night. It was too late to go into town but too early to go to bed. Douglas and I were with the boys, sitting on the edge of the stone wall next to Joaquin's house. We would be staying at his house that night, so we didn't have far to walk when we were ready for bed.

Joaquin lived here with his family. He'd never given up, praying without ceasing for God to give him a wife. They have a beautiful baby girl and lived in the house that was always meant for Joaquin. I was in Timotes visiting, but had brought gifts, of course, because their precious girl was like my own. The walk up the hill seemed longer since I hadn't been doing it every day. The people up there were the same. They love the

Lord, and they make it clear every time they see me that they still love me.

We look out over the town but mostly up at the night sky. Our same joke never got old. The boys and I would always laugh when we sat out on a dark night. High up in the air would be hundreds of lights. "Which ones are lights from houses and which ones are stars?" Jhonattan jokingly asked, obviously looking for a response from Douglas. It did make us ponder the question. When we saw those houses way up on the hillside during the day we began to wonder if Jesus was Lord over those homes. We would never know unless we met them personally. Regardless, just like all of us, they are in need of grace.

The famous lines in the hymn "Amazing Grace" describe it so beautifully: "Amazing Grace, how sweet the sound, that saved a wretch like me." One man in a small church outside Charlotte invested in me, a wretch in need of grace. His action sent me on a journey that continues to this day in these mountains. Grace comes from God, and it is so wonderful because we don't deserve it. It's also wonderful because when he shows it to us, it helps us find real life and purpose.

This páramo is by far the most beautiful place I've ever seen. It is a paradise for photographers and sightseers, and it's a joy to deal with its people. They are hospitable, pleasant, and courteous to everyone. My years living there showed me what their true beauty is. They are a picture of the love God wants us to share with others who need it. They have become my closest friends.

Over the years the boys and I talked about everything. They were curious to know about my life in New York and about different sports I participated in. That night, Evaristo told Douglas, "I remember when Mateo used to teach the kids how to play American football right back here," pointing to some vacant farmland. Evaristo was pointing out the need to continue investing in young lives here.

"Yeah, he loves sports," Douglas replied. "From what he tells me, he's good at golf, too, but I'll have to see for myself someday." Douglas and I had always talked about playing golf sometime in Caracas but hadn't had that chance. Maybe someday we will.

Douglas had heard my stories about golf, but the boys never did. When I was younger, I played in youth golf tournaments, but my love for the game grew much more than my talent level. My scores were high even though I could hit the ball a country mile off the tee. My handicap never went below ten, extremely mediocre. But hitting the ball far is fun even if it didn't lead to great scoring. I always shared with the boys about my desire to go up to the highest peak around Timotes and just tee a ball up.

"I was always curious to see how far a ball would travel in this thin air." If I'd done it ten years earlier, I may have reached a handful of homes who believed in God. Driving a ball now, I would have reached hundreds.

When I first visited Guillermo in La Puerta, there were only four or five churches in the mountains. That number is well over twenty and continues to grow. Guillermo realized the importance of investing in young people right from the start of his ministry. The most amazing thing about what I have experienced in this Andean work is with the young people here. Almost every single young person wants to be a missionary! It is like nothing I've ever seen before. I'm convinced that a great wave of international missionaries will come out of this region soon. Many churches around Venezuela have a select few kids who are highly enthusiastic about ministry, but in the mountains the number is astounding.

The boys and Douglas form a mini-congregation as they lean against the stone wall, so I start into an impromptu sermon. I tell them, "In a strategy meeting with Guillermo and some young people in La Puerta several years ago, God impressed it upon my heart to tell these young kids to start taking steps to secure a passport. Many had thought it silly when I told them this ministry would be international in a few years, but some took my word and have passports. Those without passports have missed out on opportunities to go to Argentina, Curacao, and even Mexico with Guillermo, me, and others as invitations continue to come."

Many mornings were spent out here watching the sun come up over the mountains. This was the true beauty of the paramo, seeing it with light shining on it. The young people now attending church had accepted the invitation to be part of what God was doing here. They were in the sunrise of their lives, and staying faithful to the work there, they will be used to continue to bring light to this place.

I share with the boys about a recent Facebook chat session I had with a young man from Timotes that the brothers know well. " I told him that I was meeting with pastors in Chicago to promote the work in Timotes. His response shocked me. He did not once think about what these churches could do on volunteer trips to help Timotes. His response was, 'Wow! That's such great news. God Bless those churches that are coming alongside us to reach the nations for Christ.' " My sermon continued, "He had his focus on the nations, not just his little world. His focus, just like our heavenly Father's, is to reach the nations, the entire world, not just our limited sphere of influence."

So many thoughts are going through my head now, like the human heart being a beautiful landscape, but aside from God, like the páramo. I'm on a role now, so I continue, "Until the truth of God's word penetrates our hearts, this beautiful landscape will be desolate. In many instances in the Bible God warns man to get his heart right. Getting things right with God and making him part of our lives will help make that beauty more complete. Any friendships we make have so much to offer us. The kingdom of God is filled with people from all over the world who once rejected him. They were once void of purpose and abundant life but have since received it and are sharing it with others."

Timotes is so different now and the boys have also seen its change. "Many lives have been changed in these mountains, and God's kingdom continues to grow because his obedient children are a part of what he is doing.", I add, with the boys still listening intently. " They have accepted the invitation, as I did several years ago, to explore and reside in the paramo, created by God for God, a place God loves and gave his life for."

The boys had heard many stories about what it was like to work on golf courses, but Douglas hadn't. "The farm work here would be a whole lot easier with the tractors we use on the golf course," I said changing subjects slightly, realizing it would never happen but wishing it out loud anyway.

Years ago, heading out early in the morning to a golf course with dew still it was a peaceful experience I didn't think could ever be matched. I was alone out there before the sunrise with only my thoughts and surrounded by endless acres of beauty. The peace in those moments was unreal, but in a few short years I had experiences that magnified God's overwhelming greatness and offered me an even greater peace.

I told the boys how much I'd missed this place. The most unreal experience of my life was once walking out of my house, where Joaquin lives, and looking straight up at the mountains towering over me. I was already higher up than most people ever get, and the mountains seemed to just start rising from there. It reminded me of how small we are and how big God is. I tell them, "We are so small in comparison to him, but no one is insignificant." Caught up in the magnitude of the moment, I started to get introspective and emotional.

Continuing, I recognize out loud "I can't take credit for any of the great things happening here now, but I have been witness to them. I am extremely grateful for the journey." It all started with just one person taking an interest in me so many years ago.

We were looking out over the lights of the Timotes valley. Without any sort of prompting Jhonattan asked, "All the work here started with Guillermo, huh, Mateo?" He too was impressed with everything that has happened in Timotes in a relatively short time. "God used him, that's for sure," I replied. I told them that Guillermo sadly did not live in La Puerta anymore, that he had returned to Maracaibo and was planting churches with his brother Javier. The church in Timotes, though, continued with Pastor Angel with a clear vision and is not intimidated by the task ahead. Passionate about building the rehab center to serve this population in the mountains, the church was growing and moving forward. They also hope the rehab center will be a model used all over the Andes. The other new Baptist churches in the mountains are also growing and continuing in their plans and visions.

"Lives are being impacted like never before here in the mountains," I tell the boys. "It is interesting to think back on how our work here started." I tell them the story of how that young missionary couple met Guillermo after seeing the church in La Puerta with a padlock on it. I tell them that the very same perseverance is important in relationships too.

The number of new or reconciled congregations keeps growing. In Andean towns such as La Puerta, Jajo, La Mesa de Esnujaque, Chachopo, Mucuchies, Cruz Chiquita, Zea, Pueblo Llano, and many others, we see that God is moving not just in Timotes but all over the páramo. I would be content to live out the rest of my years helping to make this list grow from La Puerta to Patagonia. I am blessed to be part of it, and having had the chance to live in this desolate place has given me life again. My faith is real; I'm not someone just going through the motions.

We sat on that stone wall for a few more minutes. People with their children walking hand in hand greeted us as they passed by. They were heading to buy food from Teofilo, who runs a store next to my old house. On rainy nights I would sit in his mini-store and listen to the rain that sounded like gravel being poured on his tin roof and watch old movies. He was a huge fan of WWE wrestling. Many things like these are mysteries until we make the effort to know people deeper than just on the surface.

We were all tired at that point but stayed out a few more minutes and chatted. The night sky was clearer than normal, and we were enjoying the lights above. We hadn't been on a hike in a while, so I asked Jhonattan when we were going again. He replied, "Mañana" in his normal, joking way. Tomorrow was not going to be possible, as I was leaving in two days, but his humor was appreciated; it made Joaquin let out the loud belly laugh he was famous for.

It made me think we could all use a little more spontaneity in our lives. If it were possible, I would have loved to have gone on a hike. I was still in good shape, but Douglas and I were soon leaving, Douglas to Caracas, and I back to the United States to the stable life there that I finally have. I had no clue when I'd be back to this magical place. There is an urgency to move many times in life, but so many times we put things off.

The boys went back to their houses. I continued staring at the lights high above, still in awe that I once lived here, in Timotes. As children we were taught about faith and how powerful it can be. I had some belief in those Bible stories we were taught back then but had developed a faith only in tangible things. My faith is a bit more profound now, and there is no doubt that I have been witness to a powerful thing in this town. I have seen these mountains move.

One of Four Original Pictures taken on Macchu Picchu hike

Caracas

...God's Protection Over his Children

Sometimes you have to publicly acknowledge that God himself saved you from harm. I am alive today because God did that for me one night. One trip I frequently made from the mountains was back to Cabimas to visit friends. If I had known what was in store for me I may have stayed home.

I had left Valera at around two in the afternoon hoping to be in Cabimas before dark. A direct trip would be no longer than four hours. Just below Valera is a national guard checkpoint that always makes me, a foreigner, nervous. Highway checkpoints are common when crossing from one state to another in Venezuela since police there do not patrol or pull cars over normally. These guards always stop buses and cars, bothering travelers for identification. They do what they want, stop whom they want; there is very little control over what they do. At different points and at different times we've been stopped at such checkpoints and have been harassed and solicited for bribes even with in-order paperwork.

I didn't remember ever having problems at this one area, but friends on the mountain have said that it was a bad one as far as having stern guards. There is nothing scarier than being half-asleep and being asked by an armed national guard officer for your cedula de identidad, identification card. It was an experience I'd had on several occasions in Venezuela, and I feared having the same thing happen to me that time, but we sailed through the checkpoint without any trouble that time. The smooth sailing didn't last long.

Our bus made stops at every house in the countryside and on almost every street corner in the towns we passed through, so by the time we got to the city next to Cabimas it was getting dark. I took a taxi to the Cabimas bus terminal, where friends were waiting for me. It was actually a porpuesto route, and two other passengers were in the car with me.

It was completely dark once we got to Cabimas. On occasion my mind drifted, and I would think and act as if I were in New York. Forgetting my surroundings, I leaned from the backseat of the taxi to the front, letting my arms hang over the seat and leaving the lights of my cell phone exposed. Before any of us knew it, the taxi was up on a curb, and all of us were against the wall with guns pointed at our heads. The police had stopped us, thinking that I was robbing the taxi driver at gunpoint. In a guilty-until-proven-innocent-culture we were all suspects until things were sorted out.

The police began to search all our belongings, and I heard everyone eyeing me and saying, "It's him over there." One cop asked me, "Where is your cedula?" I responded that it was in my backpack, and he said, "Pass it here." He looked through my belongings until he found my passport. The moments that led up to that were completely horrifying. While he was looking he kept the gun aimed squarely at me. He said, "If I find anything that resembles a weapon, I will pull the trigger."

This could not be happening to me. Anything with a sharp point or blade could be considered a weapon. I normally carried scissors for opening bags of fertilizer, and I had a small Swiss army knife in that bag. There is no earthly explanation for why the officer happened to reach into a pair of pants where my passport was before he found those other items. If he was looking for my ID, he would have been looking in a smaller pouch on the top of the backpack. The "weapons" I was carrying were in that small pouch.

He opened the large part of the bag, and under some folded clothes he found my passport. When he was finally able to confirm I was an American, he said, "You are free to go." He knew no American would be crazy enough to rob a taxi in a foreign country, so he dropped the gun and got back in his car. God stepped in that night to save me from severe harm.

It was hard to understand these horrible things affecting me one after the other. A country I loved so much appeared to be biting me as I tried to care for it. It didn't make sense, but it happens to many people, not just me. It happens to anyone who tries to bring light to dark places in this world.

... My Shortcomings

It is interesting to think that when the Great Commision in Matthew 28 tells us to "Go", it doesn't say "first, get a pHD in Theology and eliminate all of your bad habits."

The prevailing image most have of an overseas missionary is one of a spiritual giant who has no character flaws and has never done anything wrong. I am here to tell you that on the mission field, there are in fact many spiritual giants, men and women who are great examples and great encouragers to everyone they encounter. There are also a great number of people, like me, with warts and scars, still in the process of learning how to serve God effectively. Even the spiritual giants of the world have found ways to overcome their shortcomings, learning how to rely more and more on God throughout everything they face.

Douglas accompanied me to the mountains on one of my last trips to Venezuela. This was a much-needed vacation from school that Douglas was sacrificing to visit his friends in Timotes along with me. It was an inspiration to see his dedication to missions and that he was taking the work in the mountains as seriously as I was.

Whenever I travel from New York to Miami on my way to Venezuela, I see a family who has been of eternal value to me. Erwin and his wife, Reina, are from Cabimas but live near Miami, and always pick me up when I get there. They give me a meal and a place to stay, and they've always taken me to churches in the area to promote the work. It was a great two days I spent with them before I started getting ready for the international journey. There was added excitement to this trip because just days before I'd reunited through e-mail with Erika, the former English student of mine from the UCV. I'd heard that she'd gotten married and was living in Italy. She was a flight attendant with a Venezuelan airline and would be working my flight!

I was out and about buying supplies and snacks for the when Erika had called. It had been at least four years since we'd talked, so it was exciting to say the least. "I can't wait to see you!" she shouted. "Make sure you are there three hours before the flight leaves to give yourself time to get through security, and have your passport ready."

The very second she said the word "passport" my heart sank. Pale white from fear and now pacing through the aisles of a Borders bookstore, I had to respond. "I can't fly; I left my passport in my bedroom in New York." "No puede serrrr! Mateo, estas locoooo" she said in a scolding tone, basically calling me a crazed lunatic. When you're talked to in that fashion by a friend you haven't seen in four years, it's pretty serious, but I deserved every bit of it.

The possibility still existed to get the passport sent overnight, but it was chancy that I'd get it in time to fly. Reina and I started scrambling, trying magic tricks to make my passport out of thin air. I could not believe I'd made such a mistake, but it was typical of what I tended to do when I had a lot on my mind. The airline told me that there was no way to change the flight because the volume of passengers had increased for the holiday season and there was no way to get me on another flight; I would lose the money I'd spent on the airfare. It looked like I would once again fall victim to my flighty and disorganized nature, but a very resourceful and quick-acting cousin overnighted my passport.

As I was waiting to board the plane, I saw Erika walking up to me in her flight attendant's uniform. She gave me a big hug. It was especially exciting to see her since she was not expecting me to be on that flight. There had not been enough time in all the confusion the night before to let her know I'd gotten my passport after all.

"I have to go get things ready on the plane, but what row are you sitting in? I will see if they will give me that part of the plane," she said.

As I boarded, Erika told me, "Matthew, stand over here." A last-minute cancellation in first class had left a spot open. "The bad news is that they put me in the back of the plane, but the good news is this!" She motioned to my spacious seat in the front row.

Erika let the other flight attendants know I was a good friend of hers, so they treated me like royalty. A trip that could have easily become a disaster because of me was turning out to be something special despite me. This had nothing to do with anything I had done to make it good. The flight was one of the best I'd ever had to Caracas, and it even arrived on time.

Erika gave me a ride to the city and took me to my old apartment. Since it was still property of the mission board, it was being rented by my friend Elias, a pastor of a nearby church, and he allowed me to stay with him that night.

I called Dagmar first as was my custom whenever I got to Caracas, and then I called Douglas to make plans for our trip. The next day I met him in the center of town at Subway (the restaurant) and then we took a bus directly to Barquisimeto. From there we took a taxi to Cabimas, where we spent a few days before heading up the mountain to Timotes. God used Douglas and I greatly in Las Playitas, a new cell group at the upper end of Timotes.

That trip to Venezuela soon came to a close, and it was time to head back to the States. I spent the day before I left with friends, buying gifts for my family and friends. My flight to Miami had very few passengers. Erika was also on the flight, but I sat in coach that time. I remember walking toward the back of the plane during the flight and chatting with my friend and a few of her coworkers when they had free time.

Reaching the gate in Miami, I started to think of the long line that awaited me at customs and about the possibility of having my bags opened for inspection. I knew that the late hour at which we'd arrived along with the nightmare that customs always seemed to be would get me out of the airport very late. It worried me that some friends who had to work the next day would be waiting so long for me.

I hustled out of the almost-empty plane and down the hallway to a moving sidewalk toward the escalator leading to a train that took us to customs. I was making very good time and felt good about getting out of the airport at a decent hour. But in my haste I'd left several gifts behind. I attempted to call Erika, but she wasn't answering. Several hundred dollars' worth of gifts had been lost. I left a frantic voice mail for her, but she never responded.

A forgotten passport started the trip, and merchandise left behind on the plane was its end. I began to think about what Erika may be thinking about me and the fact that she'd witnessed both these events on this trip. She'd not seen how God had arranged things for me to impact this small mountain town and also a young man who was a believer because of my English outreach years ago in Caracas, so I feared she'd just focus on the glaring mistakes I seemed to make a lot. Instead, she told me over the phone a few weeks later that my love for her country had always moved her and that she wanted to start attending church. The last time I was in Venezuela she went to church with me.

Instead of focusing on the work in the mountains, sometimes I'd focus on my own problems. Erica had seen me on my worst and on my best days, but our relationship continues to grow. In developing close relationships and spending more time with people we run the risk of exposing them to our bad habits. But it also allows us to let God work through us. He is the one who will touch others' lives anyway, not us.

The catastrophe I had almost made of the trip showed me that relationships should always take priority over problems. Reflecting on things recently, I began to think about some other habits and quirks God had allowed me to eliminate and those I still have that are so evident. I also began to think about the truth that criticism comes easier than praise; it is in our nature as humans to shine more light on negative things. Even when people see just the negatives, we have to remember that God is still at work. The moment my desire to work in these mountains dies is when I will know my shortcomings are too big for God to use me here.

... Being Clay in His Hands

Many things in life do not make sense when we try to understand them on our own. When I graduated from college and started moving my way up in an exciting career, seemingly out of nowhere my plans changed. I was called to a different country and a different culture. And just as that move was starting to make sense, God set another move in motion from the largest city in Venezuela to a mountain peak with a population not even 5 percent of Caracas.

There was another ministry I was also involved in that showed the depth of need and danger in Caracas. Petare, a large barrio in the eastern part of the city, looks like a sea of shanty houses stuck to the hillside with glue; its landscape seemed to have no end. Allison was working full-time there, and her invitation to join her there one day led to an awesome opportunity. She was working with Aquilena, a seminary student from Caracas who'd begun working there to fulfill some practicum credits and had never left. Petare was a place that completely matched the image anyone would have of a mission field, and Allison loved it. I didn't understand that love at the start, but I came to love it very much as well.

Petare's subway station is wall-to-wall people from sunup to sundown. A nonstop wave of street vendors and shoppers starts at the station's exit, and there never seemed to be enough room to even walk let alone get a taxi. The sea of people seemed to move just enough to let vehicles past. Working with Allison on Fridays allowed me to get to know these people well. We'd take jeeps from the station to the heart of Petare but still had a long trip on foot ahead of us. Staircases all over this barrio connected its different parts. We would go to the top of one every Friday to meet with Luz Elena and her family.

I eventually became involved in a ministry there with some kids who wanted to form a baseball team. Every Friday I'd go to Petare with Allison, Enoch and Aquilena and meet with these kids as they headed to do visitation in other areas. We'd begin with a short Bible devotional and then head down to the ball field to practice. They'd take batting practice and I'd hit ground balls to the infielders for hours. It was a nice change from the routine of the university work but something I took very seriously.

After the sun sets in Petare, people do not want to be caught outside. One evening we'd gotten a late start with the kids, so practice ran late, and then I visited a family who had asked me to see them. I returned to the home where we had the Bible devotional as the sun was setting. Grim faces greeted me as I entered. They looked toward the door with scared looks on their faces. "Mateo, it is getting dark. You can't leave tonight. You need to stay here." They made me dinner and pulled out a mattress for me. An hour or so later I learned why they'd made me stay. I heard gunshots outside until the early hours of the morning. It sounded like a war zone. Gang activity and drug-related violence made it a very rough place, especially at night. The needs there weighed on me. I was starting to believe that this was where I was called to spend my life. In a way that few would understand, I fell in love with Petare. The people there welcomed me, and I made friends with even some gang members, who took it upon themselves to protect me. The needs in this place were hundredfold. The workers there, unfortunately, were few.

I considered New York City, just over an hour from where I'd grown up, and all the needs there. It would not be a far-fetched idea to think that I could be a missionary to that city so close, a place of endless danger and anguish. Trips to New York would be cheaper and more frequent.

I also could have stayed in New Jersey to work with the small Bible study group. The Hispanic population all over the United States is ever growing, along with the need to reach out to them. My travels have taken me to large cities and to desolate mountain peaks. I have seen that the God of Times Square is also the God of desolate places. He has created all things for his pleasure. We can do a lot of good things in life, but we do the best thing when we follow God's plan even when it doesn't seem to make sense.

There is no way I will ever understand why things worked out in my life for me to leave one of the most highly populated cities in Latin America to work in a small farming community with fewer visible needs. That answer will not be fully answered here on earth, but what I learned in the months and years contemplating this question is the greatest lesson God has taught me.

Up on the mountain working on the farms, or even on the golf course, soil testing is very important. The fertility of a soil can be checked many times by just taking a handful and inspecting it visually. Many a time would I grab a handful of clay or sand and just let it sift through my fingers.

I am clay in God's hands. He can do whatever he wants to do with my life, but whatever he chooses to do will always be to prosper and to bless me. The years I spent in Venezuela have taught me something about relationships, but the most important relationship in life is with our Creator. Our relationship with him should lead us to trust him more every day, even when we don't understand exactly how he is working out his purpose for our lives.

La Puerta (from Pueblo Nuevo)

Timotes